NO-NONSENSE PLANNING

No-Nonsense Planning

Richard S. Sloma

THE FREE PRESS
A Division of Macmillan, Inc.
NEW YORK

Collier Macmillan Publishers
LONDON

This book is dedicated, with love,
to my daughters, Lynn and Karen.
Even if I could *have used*
"no-nonsense planning,"
I couldn't be more proud of them
or love them more.

Copyright © 1984 by The Free Press
A Division of Macmillan, Inc.

The Free Press
A Division of Macmillan, Inc.
866 Third Avenue, New York, N. Y. 10022

Collier Macmillan Canada, Inc.

Printed in the United States of America

printing number

1 2 3 4 5 6 7 8 9 10

Library of Congress Cataloging in Publication Data

Sloma, Richard S.
  No-nonsense planning.

  Includes index.
  1. Corporate planning.   I. Title.
HD30.28.S54   1984   658.4'012   84–13647
ISBN 0–02–929520–3

Contents

v

Preface

This book provides essential insights into the mentality required for successful, effective planning. Library shelves are filled with "cookbook" approaches to planning, which myopically focus on the tools and techniques that planners use. They erroneously lead managers to the conviction that "completing the plan" is a legitimate end, whereas the effective manager "knows" that the plan itself is but a tool in the management toolbox. While it is undeniably an important tool, perhaps *the* most important, it is, alas, only a tool.

This book will stretch the imagination and understanding of the reader by exploring the psychological underpinnings of the planning process itself. Careful study of it will reveal how an effective manager "knows" that the plan is, itself, but a tool in the management toolbox. This book will enable the reader to plan the plan and to control the completion of the plan no matter which of the planning techniques, forms, or formats are used.

Finally, and probably most important, the last chapter presents an unprecedented planning approach to achieving any managerial objective—the Human PERT Chart. In recognition that the effective manager is one who gets excellent results through the efforts of others, the Human PERT Chart provides a sure-fire process to accurately assess and control the attitudes and inclinations of the people who may influence the outcome of your effort to achieve a specific goal or objective.

This book is not aimed at the carpenter-managers who are engrossed with their saws and hammers; it is aimed at the architect-and-developer managers who take the broad view of the business. It is aimed at general managers and those who aspire to be general managers.

Introduction

The need for business planning is too extensively demonstrated by the prevalence of planning functions in business organizations today to require justification here. Perhaps the most succinct summary of this need can be expressed as follows: Lip service is always paid to the proposition that one of the prime functions of top management is to plan. Yet in too many companies the failure to fulfill this obligation adequately and rigorously is excused by the rationalization that there are just too many day-to-day problems that must be solved, too many "fires" that must be put out. "After all," we hear, "if we don't take care of today, there just won't be a tomorrow." My response is that *the extent of involvement by top management in day-to-day problems is directly proportional to lack of judicious delegation to second-level and beyond.*

Further, it is my conviction that lack of delegation is in turn caused by a lack of organizational "confidence" that all management personnel are moving in the same direction—toward the same goals, in the same order of priority, and at the same pace. Finally, the lack of "confidence" exists because the individual manager has not been provided with a "frame of reference" within which he can make decisions. He and other management personnel have not been provided with a conceptualization of the role they play in achieving the corporate goal. *They have not been provided with (or, better yet, participated in the preparation of) a "Plan."*

Most typically, the result of business planning in any firm resolves itself into quantitative evaluation of only one of the many feasible alternative courses of action available to, or enforced upon, the firm's management. Why is this so?

We may arrive at the answer to this question by first looking at the preferred approach to the planning process. First of all, the reasonable available alternatives must be identified. Then they must be reduced to projected financial figures, that is, the series of functional plans that must be prepared to yield the end result or the pro forma balance sheet. In each of the plans is embedded a perhaps large, but nevertheless finite, number of feasible alternatives, which *should* be evaluated to provide management with meaningful assistance.

Never forget that the planning process is an iterative dynamic. Through its iterative course, adjustments of parameters in conformity with probability of occurrence will lead to different end results. The useful—i.e., effective—plan will explore all the reasonably probable parameter values with judicious ranges of value.

For example, the Sales Plan should explore decision

alternatives concerning product mix, prices, volumes, and other aspects. Some of these, e.g. the abandonment of a product, are under control of management. Some are subject to "battle" conditions in the market, e.g. local price warfare. In any event, each of these significant alternatives should be evaluated at various values to quantify their impact on the projected balance sheet.

The real need for effective business planning, then, is to provide that "frame of reference" within which delegated decision-making authorities can be confidently made; to eliminate the continuance of *ad hoc,* from-the-hip definitions of goals and decision criteria, which at best offer only short-term expedience to the detriment of long-term management organization development. *For it is widely accepted that the most significant factor distinguishing "good" companies from "excellent" companies is the thoroughness with which the solidarity of the management team is established, nurtured, and developed.* Finally, it is axiomatic that the shortfall of maximum return to the shareholders/owners can be accurately measured by the extent to which there is failure to document meaningful business plans.

What is deserving of some amplification, however, is the answer to the question, "What is *effective* business planning?" Business planning has variable meaning, depending upon which function of the firm is considered and with which management echelon within that function we are concerned. For the purposes of the presentation in the following pages, we shall consider business planning only from the topmost management level, from the viewpoint of the firm. If we can contribute toward a solution at this level, lower management level solutions will thereby present themselves.

Business planning at the top management level should comprise an attempt to evaluate the impact on the projected income statement and balance sheet of alternative courses of policy action and alternative industry responses to market behavior.

Thus in all of the functional plans, many alternatives should be available quantitatively for management scrutiny.

When one considers the mountainous and tedious arithmetic workload faced in reducing a set of management policy and action alternatives to the projected financial statements, there is little wonder that typically only one set of alternatives (or a few at best) is explored, evaluated, and made available for management decision-making.

Largely because of the large volume of fifty-grade arithmetic necessary to evaluate alternatives, top management is denied the assistance it deserves and needs.

If management in a firm is to accomplish effective business planning thoroughly, two obstacles must be economically overcome:

1. Quantitative definition of probable alternatives
2. The ensuing arithmetic workload to evaluate each alternative

Clearly, any business planning technique that can offer solutions to these two problems allows management the opportunity to evaluate systematically, in predetermined increments and decrements, several series of alternatives. Business planning assumes the form of a "movie," a series of "stills" in rapid, orderly, and predetermined motion. Business planning becomes dynamic.

The very essence of effective business planning lies in an ability to pretest a plan before it is implemented in the "real world." Traditionally, the only practical test put to a plan was an "after-the-fact" test; actual performance (if quantitatively measured at all) was compared to the plan on a historical basis. If criteria are met, the plan is "successful," and vice versa. In "Pre-Test Your Long-Range Plans" (*Harvard Business Review,* January–February 1959, pp. 119–27), W. J. Platt and N. R. Maines discuss in detail the role of management science in effective business planning. They sum it up: "A company must have some experimental means by which to make its planning mistakes inexpensively."

NO-NONSENSE
PLANNING

PART I

The Twenty Basic Principles of Planning

PRINCIPLE 1

Recognize Planning for What It Is—and Is Not

Planning has often been described as a thankless, inglorious task. If we are going to reach an effective, useful understanding of "planning," we must first get straight that "planning" is NOT a task or an event. *Planning is first and foremost an attitude, a frame of mind.*

Each of us from time to time has marveled at someone or other who has a way of "cutting through all the B.S. and getting right to the heart of the problem." Anyone who shows that talent is a genuine, natural-born planner. *The prime attribute of successful planning is the ability to identify quickly an end result acceptable to the affected parties.* The degree of ability of a person to envision quickly but thoroughly the dimensions of an acceptable outcome is what measures his performance as a planner.

It is almost always the case that if a person can quickly and accurately assess the circumstantial evidence and identify the goal or the constraint, he will be eminently

3

able to document the steps required to reach that goal or loosen that constraint.

Successful planning requires also *the ability to approach an undefined situation in an orderly "C-to-B-to-A" manner.* No, I did not mean "A to B to C"! CBA is *not* a misprint. "CBA" is the first and most important insight needed to graduate into the ranks of a "professional" planner. It means that you *start* at the point at which you want to *end,* then walk backward across the time-bridge, one step at a time, until you arrive at the present. Much more will be said about this essential mental attitude later.

The bridge needed to reach from the desired circumstances back to the present circumstances must be built on a brick-by-brick basis, with the firm mortar of close reasoning in between.

While it is necessary that planning be approached with conquering enthusiasm, it is equally necessary that the planner remain consummately dispassionate. Failure to remain objective leaves a planner with only wished-for results rather than a realistic appraisal of an achievable result.

Planning is a process. It is a dynamic process in that daily events will affect the plan's viability either favorably or otherwise. Planning is *not* an event or exercise culminating in a nicely bound book to be placed on a shelf and forgotten after surviving the obligatory "dog-and-pony" show that must (alas!) be put on for the "brass."

The plan, the set of physical documents that explain the intended action, is but the best estimation of the timing sequence and fulfillment of intended actions. In that respect plans are always "wrong," because the future will never unfold precisely as we plan it. At the same time they are always "right" in that they should always reflect the best, most current thinking and evaluation at the time of their formation.

While plans by their very nature are transitory and short-lived, they are nonetheless commitments to measured performance. It is upon plans that budgets are constructed. It is upon budgets that banking and financial relationships are pegged. Thus plans and planning are serious stuff indeed. Credibility of management and individuals' careers rest precariously on excellence in forecasting. Sometimes it's referred to as "keeping your word."

Planning is a participatory activity. That is to say, effective, successful planning is a participatory activity. Too often one sees in business organizations that planning has been assigned to an individual. "He's in charge of planning," whatever the hell that means. Unfortunately the designee is usually a staff member of some sort and "coordinates" or "leads" the planning effort. *But planning is a process, not an "effort."* It cannot be performed well if entrusted to a staff person or group who remain invulnerable to the risk of performance failure.

Responsibility for planning activity belongs *only* in the line organization. It is as much an element of the job description of any line manager as is his functional responsibility. Yet too often we hear, "I don't have time to *plan;* I have to get to *work.*" Absolute nonsense! "Never mind the reentry point. Hell, let's just launch the capsule." Any superior who tolerates that attitude in his subordinates should keep his résumé current.

Making a road map, planning has been called. Well,

perhaps there's something to it, but clearly not nearly as much as one would like to think. In planning the variables shift and sway. Not only do landmarks appear, disappear, and change appearance, but the roads themselves appear, disappear, and change direction. Planning requires going over the premises, assumptions, performance, and goals again and again; it is an *iterative process*. Each time you perform an iteration, you learn a little more about the challenge; it is a heuristic process.

Perhaps, at bottom, it is the requirement of continuous dedication, care, and attention to detail that most managers find unappealing about planning. They must find something unappealing, because there are so many managers who do a lousy job of planning.

Certainly a major if not principal cause of the widespread poor performance is the confusion between the "how" of completing the plan and the "why" one does planning at all. The jargon of software and the arcane symbolic language of operations research, with its mathematical formulas, no doubt polish the allure of being one of the "initiated." Too many otherwise bright and capable people become irretrievably caught up in the mechanics of planning and, to enhance their "profession" (and their personal ego) set a higher priority on polished algorithms than on achievement of the plan objectives.

Too often—far too often—the so-called planners focus exclusively on the "how to" aspects of planning and disregard the "what for." Our business schools, both at undergraduate and graduate levels, lead aspiring managers down the primrose path of pursuit of false precision. To quantify alone increases neither the validity nor the "doability" of the finished plan.

One is constantly reminded of the dedicated "professional" engineer who keeps fussing with possible ways to read a slide rule to four decimal places, when design tolerances can accommodate variations of plus/minus a quarter of an inch. In short, the purpose of planning is *not* to glorify the process but to make money for the owners of the firm.

PRINCIPLE 2

Go for the Jugular!

A crucially important mental prerequisite for successful, effective planning is unswerving dedication to relentless pursuit of *the* critical, pivotal, key objective. Never lose sight of the goal! Sift through the circumstances, opinions, documents and "facets" until you are absolutely certain that you have identified the linchpins. Then do NOT lose sight of them.

If you play chess, you probably learned how in precisely the opposite sequence from the sequence in which you should have learned. You most probably started with the openings—even bought some books and all, did you? Tsk, tsk! After learning how to avoid Fool's Checkmate, you jumped to the middle game. Also you started to play more frequently, "Nothing like 'cross the board' combat," and all that. Your won–loss ratio was probably pretty bad. Finally you started to pay attention to the end game. The more you played, the more your won–

loss ratio improved—not because you controlled the game better by enforcing your will on your opponent, but because you screwed up less frequently. And so you too entered the ranks of the mediocre woodpushers.

What you did wrong was to approach the game the way Alice suggested: You started at the beginning and so forth. To be really successful at chess, as at business planning, don't even think about the beginning *until you really know where you want to wind up. You start always at the end!* That way, you always know that you are proceeding toward the goal that you're really after. There are fewer than 150 ways to checkmate your opponent's king and win the game. So the most effective way to learn chess is to learn the end game first so that you can quickly recognize the mating patterns. Next, study the middle game to learn how to force your opponent into an already familiar end game position. Finally, study the opening game to learn how to force your opponent into a known middle game position that leads, in turn, to a winning end game pattern. Always go immediately for the jugular; it's the most effective way to save a lot of time and effort.

To be a successful planner, go thou and follow the same sequence! Start at the end, whether the "end" is a date, a dollar amount, a technical performance specification, a personnel action, or whatever. If you can't definitively state ahead of time what the desired end result is, you should not even begin to put together what you may call a plan, because you will fail.

Once you can define clearly, quantitatively, and succinctly the end or goal or objective, you can begin to ask the only two questions you will ever need:

1. What has to happen immediately prior for that result to occur?
2. How likely is it that the prerequisite event or set of circumstances will occur?

That's all there is to it. Big deal! Once you can answer those two questions about the goal, ask them again of the next immediately preceding event or circumstance, and so on until you are all the way back to the present, to today. Thus, having identified and positioned all of the intermediate dominoes, you can confidently tip the first one, secure in the knowledge of when and where the last one will fall. The reason you ask the second question, often overlooked by planners, is that it affords you assurance that no intervening causal step has been overlooked.

The more you practice this "last is first" principle, the more proficient you will become. And—guess what!—sooner than you would imagine, it will be natural for you to think in anticipatory terms. You will be able more and more quickly to ennumerate the intervening steps while your colleagues are still trying to figure out where to begin or are mired in some undefined intermediate morass.

And the oddest part of it all is that, upon even cursory consideration, it makes plain old common sense to plan in just that way.

PRINCIPLE 3

Knock It Apart—Then Put It Back Together

The more formal rendition would be: First anatomize, then synthesize. *Planning consists of linking together the steps that lead to the desired end.* Most plans are ineffective as monitoring and control devices because (1) the identified steps are too large; that is, they contain unplanned, hence uncontrollable, substeps within them, and (2) the intervening steps are largely ill-defined and all too frequently arranged in an incorrect sequence.

Effective planning, resulting in an effective plan, requires very careful consideration of the definition of the action or event steps. *The smaller the quantum of work and the less major the event, the more useful (i.e., effective) is the definition of intermediary steps.*

No plan has yet been documented, nor will one ever be, that is ineffective because the intermediary steps have been defined too narrowly, too finitely, in too much detail.

The mental set to be adopted at this initial stage in the planning process is that of the prosecutor preparing for trial, seeking a conviction based solely on circumstantial evidence. The task he faces, essentially, is to build, data point by data point, a bridge for the jury to traverse leading from the presumption of innocence to a finding of guilt beyond a reasonable doubt. The bridge must be constructed carefully lest the prosecutor lose credibility with the jury by asking them to make too large a conclusionary jump—from being seen at the scene of the crime, say, to having committed the crime.

The principle involved is that the plan must be credible both to those to whom it is presented for approval and to those who are committed to its execution. The greater the detail, the smaller the quantum of work, and the lesser the scope of the event, the greater the credibility of the plan.

This need for patient, brick-by-brick tearing down and building is what causes many people to find planning a tedious chore indeed. Their mental impatience and their short attention span drive them to "get on with it."

Careful attention to keeping the plan elements as small as practical has great benefit. During anatomization it guarantees that you have not overlooked crucial even though minor steps. And during synthesization relatively small work increments are much easier to arrange and rearrange, much as the use of one idea per index card helps the speaker to organize his speech better.

One final point: Anatomization, if diligently performed, will ensure that you will understand the subtle intracacies of the plan better than anyone else. *This knowledge monopoly can be translated into authority.* More will be said about the organizational power potential of effective planning in Part II of this book.

PRINCIPLE 4

Always Plan with Events, Never with Processes

For crucial reasons presented later in this book, the only way effective control can result from effective planning is by the use of "events" as the quanta or building blocks of the plan. To have any chance for successful implementation, the progress toward the goal must be measurable. Ideally, the milestones will embrace both time and dollars. But there is no better measurement or control of time than a scheduled event.

An example will help get the notion across. One of the most frequently used planning exercises is the new product introduction plan. Far too often the intermediary steps are described in terms of activity rather than the event. It is not uncommon to observe the use of such plan elements as "feasibility review," "state-of-the-art search," "bread-board design," and so on. While on the one hand these activities must usually be performed in some form or another, they are useless for managerial control purposes. Much more effective are "submittal of feasibility analysis," "submittal of state-of-the-art evaluation," "completion of evaluation of bread-board prototype testing," and so on.

It is more normal for people to envision future work in terms of activities rather than events. Days (and too often, minds) are far more filled with activities than with events. Effective planning, merely by the prudent selection of measurement quanta, helps those performing the tasks to do them more effectively by *reorientation of focus from effort to results.*

Allowing activities to be used as the planning quanta allows use of totally useless measuring sticks such as "man-weeks." The use of these amorphous measuring sticks allows, in turn, the escape from accountability of the very people upon whom successful event achievement is dependent. The likelihood of plan success will have been erased.

PRINCIPLE 5

Focus on the Increment of Change

In an earlier book, *No-Nonsense Management* (Macmillan, 1977), I elaborated on the principle, "Don't expect changes in results if you haven't changed the conditions." The point in that book was that it is the manager's job to control change, to make it orderly. That change *will* occur is a given; that progress will be made is up to the manager—*you!*

The point in this book is that an effective plan provides the manager with the tool he needs to quantify, identify, isolate, and assign individual responsibility for each of the changes he seeks to make. In short, an effective plan enables a manager to control change, to make it orderly.

A plan is a series of steps that provide the means for the firm to go "from here to there." Be mindful that "here" comprises one set of operating circumstances or conditions. "There" comprises another and necessarily different set of operating circumstances and conditions.

15

An effective plan will quantitatively define and measure the differences in incremental changes, in circumstances and conditions.

The most effective way for a manager to conserve his time and that of his organization is first to rank the planned incremental changes in order of achievement complexity, and second to keep his attention (and that of this organization) focused on that list to ensure that the "toughest" changes are addressed first to avoid crippling "surprises" later on. Don't forget to rank them also by return on shareholder investment. They would like to know that you're always thinking of them.

If properly defined, the planning "steps," the incremental changes, represent the cutting edge of the manager's attempt to sculpt the future.

This principle will be dealt with in considerably greater detail in Part IV, "How to Plan an Ongoing Business." I leave you with these thoughts, borrowed from *No-Nonsense Management:*

> Results, financial and otherwise, are only the consequences of the action and interaction of forces. Some of these forces—people, products, plant, and policies—are under your direct control. [p. 67]

> The array of people, products, plant, and policies which you inherited produced certain results. Those results will be repeated in the short term if the array remains the same. But performance will erode in the long term if the array remains unchanged. [p. 68]

PRINCIPLE 6

Always Plan for Failure

Murphy's Law has not yet been repealed. If something can go wrong, it will. Robert Burns grasped this business principle about two hundred years ago. He, of course, stated it more elaborately, "The best laid schemes o' mice and men gang aft a-gley." To ignore this reality is to ensure failure. So don't ignore it!

Rather, make it the cornerstone of your planning process whenever you are planning a new venture, whether a new business or new product. Planning for failure is most useful when the program requires continuing investment, as distinguished from an episodic investment. An example of the first type is launching or "bootstrapping" a new business. The clearest example of the second type is a capital investment in a new machine tool.

Bootstrapping a new business requires ongoing (and generally increasing) investments in working capital, sales and promotion, and so on. Putting the organization in place usually costs a lot more than originally envisioned. Also, usually the cost of organization (whether technical, administration, distribution, or production) is not really dealt with for what it is, an ongoing investment.

Also, all too often the bootstrappers fail to maintain a professional objectivity with regard to their offspring. As demands for further funds arise, emotionalism tends to blur the no-nonsense scrutiny that should be provided. How do you avoid that unhappy eventuality? Simply by insistence on definition of plan alternatives, which include failure.

Prior to launch, define and quantify the circumstances under which the program will be aborted and no further good money will be thrown after bad. When dealing with the initiation of a new business, probably the most effective (both objective and easily measurable) trigger is *gross margin content in forward aged order intake*. Until the business is confirmed as viable by the capture of acceptably profitable volume, efforts to reduce "expenses" are at best a poor use of irreplacable management time and at worst may cause the demise of the program. *It is impossible to "make" profit by expense reduction!* The very best that can result from expense reduction is a preservation of profit captured at the gross margin (or standard margin) line.

Gross margin content in forward aged order intake is the earliest lead indicator of the eventual fate of the venture. Pay attention to it. Predetermine what that number must be at relevant milestones to keep your firm alive. If the actual profit content fails to meet those milestones, liquidation or disposition plans, completed earlier, should be triggered. The adverse impact on the owners will be minimized in direct proportion to the thoroughness with which failure was planned.

Part III contains a much more detailed elaboration of the application of this principle.

PRINCIPLE 7

Planning Ensures Execution

How many times have you heard frustrated and exasperated managers exhort their subordinates to improve "execution"? "We really need to execute better." "Our major stumbling block is unsatisfactory execution." Of course, execution can always be better. It's like a woman's work—it's never really done! But let us understand something about "execution": I don't know of a single firm that failed because of lousy execution. Execution is a relative term. It needs closer definition to be analytically useful.

When the statement is made that "execution was poor," there is a presumption that it could have been better. There is a further presumption that the performance achieved was somehow less acceptable than another level of performance that *could* have been achieved. Criticism of execution is warranted only when two conditions exist: First, the performance standard to which actual performance is compared is both predetermined and measura-

20

ble; second, the actual performance achieved is measured in terms that are in consonance with the standard measurements. In other words, if the predetermined performance standard is a date by which certain events must be completed, the actual performance must similarly be judged by the actual date achieved. To ignore the date achieved and fault execution because "too much expense was incurred" is not only an irrelevant measure, it is an indictment of faulty standard-setting.

All this talk about predetermined and measurable milestones is really the long way around to saying "plan." After all, that's what a plan is.

Execution is largely under management control. The shorter the control cycle, the more measurable the performance, and the more objective and impersonal the control points, the greater the degree to which meaningful management control can be exercised. In short, the more thorough and the more professional the plan that is documented prior to "execution," the greater the likelihood of achieving the plan goals. Without a plan, execution will always be faulty and unacceptable. Results will always be less than those expected—or perhaps hoped for is the more accurate term.

With a plan, the prospects for effective management control have risen exponentially. The more effective the management control, the more likely that results will meet or exceed planned results. Execution will be applauded.

The next time you hear an official bemoan "execution" by the organization, ask immediately to what extent that official championed the planning process and insisted on preparation of detailed, exhaustive plans prior to approving initiation of execution!

PRINCIPLE 8

Plan Only That to Which the Owners Are Favorably Disposed

There is absolutely no sense at all in pursuing courtship and proposal if you *know* that the girl will say no. There is absolutely no sense at all in investing your precious time in developing a plan that you *know* the "owners" *will* turn down. There is not even any sense at all in developing a plan that the "owners" will probably turn down. An early law school lesson is, "Don't ask a question if you're not sure what the answer will be." To paraphrase, "Don't present a plan if you're not sure that it will be favorably (even if perhaps critically) received."

What an obvious principle! Yes, it is obvious once you think about it a little. Yet how many times have you witnessed a premature or irrelevant presentation? To the presentor, his plan may very well be the greatest thing since sliced bread. But if the presentee is uninterested, both the plan and the presentor will go nowhere in the organization.

A plan represents, and even causes, change. All of us are familiar with the truism that people tend to resist change. For some reason, there is an unfounded presumption that "people" means "subordinates." Not so! Often it is the "superiors" who are the least flexible. All too often, their preoccupation with avoidance of making waves is cloaked in the seemingly noble garb of avoiding imagined and speculative downside risk. After all, they argue, the (execution of the) plan may not really achieve its stated objectives. As human beings, it is not abnormal for them to fear that subordinates are outstripping them, that changes are overtaking them. Maybe so, but it sure is abnormal behavior for a professional manager.

Another cause of uninterest is a mismatch, between presentor and presentee, of basic approach to the business. Say that the presentor is a "steward of corporate assets" and presents a detailed, exhaustive plan to reduce administrative expense or to control inventory better in a firm already profitable with an inventory turn on cost of 4.5. Suppose that the presentee is a true entrepreneur, a risk-taker, a deal-maker who seeks to double (or more) the value of his shareholdings. The outcome of the presentation is easily predictable. Chances are the presentor will never complete his presentation. If he does, he may, amidst the presentee's yawns and fidgets, obtain some kind of go-ahead. One thing is sure: The presentee will not be enthralled the next time he learns that the presentor is gearing up to present another plan.

In sum, ascertain as carefully as you can what the objectives of the owners are, and then formulate plans to achieve them!

PRINCIPLE 9

Never Plan "Small" Enterprises

Putting an effective plan together requires a great deal of thought, effort, and concentration. It really takes "premium" time, a personal investment of that most precious of all resources—*time*. Because *time* can never be recaptured, it must be used with extreme care and in impact priority activities.

Because effective planning places heavy demands on your time, don't become so enamored with the planning process and planning techniques that you lose time by thoughtless investment. Don't become so mesmerized by the "how" that you forget the all-important "WHY"!

Every business, at every stage of its life, faces numerous problems and opportunities. The ultimate objective of effective management is to enhance the enduring value of the shareholder's investment. Sort through the array of problems and opportunities facing a firm to identify those which have or will have substantial impact on the

24

enduring value of the shareholders' investment. Next, rank them by size or impact on the enduring value of the shareholders' investment. Finally, devote as much time as possible to formulating plans that correspond, in sequence, to the top ten.

The difference in time and effort expenditure to formulate a "high-impact plan" is not much greater than the time and effort expenditure required to formulate a "low-impact plan." The real difference is the significantly greater beneficial effect for the firm—and, of course, for you!

A great deal more will be said about this Principle in Part II.

PRINCIPLE 10

Plans Are Self-Fulfilling Prophecies

Plans are always self-fulfilling prophecies. Performance is directly related to the extent to which they are professionally prepared. With planning, the ancient adage is more true than in other contexts: You get from the activity what you put into the activity. An apathetic, unenthusiastic approach to planning will lead to the predictably dismal results that would eventuate from any activity similarly approached.

A poorly prepared plan will generate poor results. A well-prepared plan will yield good results. A professionally prepared plan will yield excellent results. It's as simple as that!

In nutrition it is often said that "you are what you eat." In business it is not often enough said that "you will be what you plan." *There is no escape from planning.* Even if you decide not to plan, you have just stated a plan—namely that all situations will be dealt with in an *ad hoc,* "shoot-from-the hip" manner. The prophecy will be fulfilled. Decisions will be made. They will certainly be inconsistent, probably counterproductive. Most will probably be bad, and the firm will soon be facing a terminal case of chaos.

On the other hand a well-documented, thoroughly prepared plan will provide the documented framework for rapid and accurate organizational communication, well identified milestones and parameters for easy group reference, a constancy of focus, and a means for effecting orderly change.

PRINCIPLE 11

The Smaller the Planned Steps, the Better

The worst way to begin a journey of a thousand steps is to try and cover it with one big step! The worst way to plan a new product is to place the order for the equipment that you think you will need to produce it. Think of planning as a prosecutor thinks of preparing a case on circumstantial evidence. The mere fact that the suspect had bloodstains on his sleeve that matched the blood type of the deceased doesn't, *by itself,* mean that the suspect was the killer. The prosecutor knows that he could never get the jury to take that big a conclusionary step. The testimony of an eyewitness placing the suspect near the scene of the crime does not, *by itself,* give the prosecutor a winning case. The fact that the suspect benefited significantly from the death of the victim does not, *by itself,* mean that the jury will convict. And so on and so on. Eventually, and with enough links in the chain, the jury will face up to the final conclusion: Given *all* of these data points, *all* these steps, *all* these facts, there can be no other credible explanation.

When you present your plan, your jury is not your peers—it's your superiors. But your task is essentially the same. You must get them to believe that there is no credible action to take other than what you propose to do. So lead them the same way a successful prosecutor does, step by step—not too big a step at any one time in the sequence, or you'll lose them.

A detailed plan demonstrates considerable forethought. Further, as you anticipate the questions and concerns of your management "jury," be sure to cover them adequately in a step-by-step, thorough manner. There is only one planning flaw that is fatal: taking *so* big a step between planning events in the sequence that the chain of credibility stretches, erodes, and finally breaks. While impatience may sometimes be registered by your management jurists because of the abundance of step and substep detail, *no plan has ever been rejected because it was too detailed!* Nor will one ever be!

So much for your "superiors." Why are small planning steps useful when dealing with "subordinates"? As will be developed in some detail in Part II, the larger the number of accountable steps, the stronger *your* entrenchment *as* a superior. Further, the greater the measurable detail of each step, the easier are your managerial tasks to control organization behavior and to exercise the organizational power needed to execute the plan successfully.

PRINCIPLE 12

Relevant Approximations Are Better than Inconsequential Minute Measurements

Always remember that no plan will ever be approved if the reviewer doesn't feel there is high probability of success. Therefore, first and foremost a plan must impress the reviewer first, that likely alternatives or scenarios have been considered, and second, that the plan is *reasonable*.

A plan deals with the future, of course. Not only can no one guarantee the future, but no one can even predict, forecast, or plan the future with accurate precision. Consequently, every number presented in the plan will be "wrong." That is, it will be inaccurate. And the farther distant the projection, the more inaccurate it is likely to be. The planner knows (or should know) this; the reviewer knows (or should know) this too.

Effective planners try not to pinpoint projections with discrete precision. They "bracket" the highly likely result by evaluation of "optimistic/pessimistic" alternatives. They use ranges. Occasionally they also present a third scenario, usually called "likely." This alternative invariably lies somewhere between "optimistic" and "pessimistic." Again, usually it is this "likely" alternative upon which justification of the plan is based.

If the downside or "pessimistic" alternative has been thoroughly explored and addressed *and* the argument that the "likely" alternative will probably occur is well presented, the plan's approval is assumed.

The reviewer will have been impressed that the anticipated results will indeed eventuate somewhere around the "likely" projection. It is not important or pivotal that projected return on investment is presented as 26.8735 percent! It is important only that the reviewer be persuaded that actual return will be somewhere between 24 and 27 percent (!), but certainly above 20 percent.

If your presentation focuses on how carefully and scientifically you measured that fourth decimal, the reviewer will certainly applaud your "professionalism"—but he will most likely reject your plan!

PRINCIPLE 13

Master the Planning Process Modules

The planning process is modular. Sometimes the modules are called subroutines. But whether you call them modules or subroutines, they are self-contained patterns of thought that are used over and over again. Mastery is not difficult; there are really only two you need! You will see them repeated over and over again in this book, and, if you plan effectively, you will use them time and time again. The first module, PNP, means Prose, Numbers, People.

In Part III of this book you will see the PNP formulation in use:

1. Formalize survival strategy

   ↓

2. Quantify survival test

   ↓

3. Quantify organizational
   performance standards

This three-step module consists first, of committing to paper your rationale, concepts, ideas, major elements, and so on in prose. You want to express the fundamental aims in writing before you attempt to quantify them. Until you can express them cogently and succinctly, your understanding of them is incomplete.

The second step is to quantify the prose. Quantification can, as we know, be expressed in dollars, dates, or physical amounts—pounds, square feet, and so forth. The third step is to translate the quantification into an action assignment to one specific individual to pinpoint responsibility and ease monitoring and control.

The PNP module always occurs before the plan is put into action! The second module, "MOOD," always occurs *after* the plan is put into action. The "MOOD" steps are as follows:

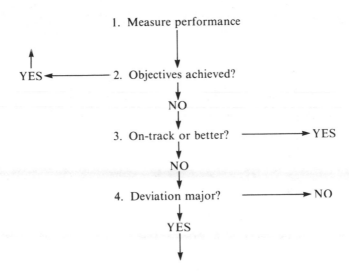

1. Measure performance

YES ◄——————— 2. Objectives achieved?

NO

3. On-track or better? ——————► YES

NO

4. Deviation major? ——————► NO

YES

Step 1 consists of measurement of actual performance achieved at meaningful intervals or milestones. The second step compares the actual performance to the predetermined objectives. Only three outcomes need concern us as managers. First, if the objectives were achieved, we should go back and reassess the objectives. The implication, of course, is that higher objectives should be set. Second, are we progressing according to plan even though the objectives have not yet been hit? If so, we should continue with plan implementation. Third, is there a major unfavorable deviation from plan? If not, let's proceed to implement the plan further. If there is a major unfavorable deviation, however, we need to implement corrective action.

Don't even begin to read Part III until you have made PNP and MOOD part of your second nature.

PRINCIPLE 14

Don't Set Objectives That Can't Be Monitored

It is generally accepted that plan objectives should always be quantified. But never fail to be mindful that once the plan is put into action, effective management control depends upon being able to compare actual performance with those objectives!

Once again, the need to anticipate is critical. In other words the capability of the actual performance reporting system must be borne in mind at the time plan objectives are quantified. A plan objective is worse than useless if actual performance progress to that objective cannot be tracked! That is not to say that quantification of plan objectives must be limited to only those measurement systems which happen to be in place. Not at all. New or modified measurement systems can be installed prior to plan execution. But, unless the actual-to-plan measurement system is analyzed and anticipated *prior to launch,* effective management control is at best in jeopardy and, at worst, nonexistant.

The actual-to-plan measurement system need not, in fact *should* not, be limited to data available through the accounting system. Wherever and whenever possible select measurements from the real, physical world. Better than sales volume *dollars,* subject to pricing, discount, and commission decisions, are *units* of sale. When assessing administrative workload, better than, say, order intake *dollar* volume, subject to wide variations in dollars-per-order, is the *number* of orders processed. Even better is number of orders processed adjusted for some measure of complexity of order. In assessment of production workload, better than work in process inventory *dollars* is the *number* of work orders issued by department.

In summary, the more compatible the quantified expression of the objective is with the feedback performance measurement system, the more effective will be monitoring and control, and the more likely it is that your plan will be successfully executed.

PRINCIPLE 15

Planning Gets Time on Your Side

There is no question but that "time" is the most valuable asset you possess. And there is no question but that the most difficult and elusive objective of professional management is the optimal use of time. The march of time is relentless. Each tick of the clock, each passing day brings the firm closer yet to the end of the month, the quarter, the year. The questions become more difficult because they become simpler. Were orders obtained or not? Were shipments made or not? Were profits made or not? Was cash flow positive or negative?

Time will be "up" and there will be no more time left. But time is *not* an enemy! It is an impersonal natural phenomenon. It is available equally to all. Time cares not which events take place or fail to take place during its passing. It is an endless belt on which events (or non-events) are transported from "We really should do . . ." to "I wish we had done. . . ."

Every program, every project, every undertaking has its own gestation period during which it is transformed from concept to result. What makes it difficult for managers is that there is no uniformity, no "standard" gestation period. Because each program, project, or undertaking touches different people or some of the same people but in different ways, each is unique. There is simply no predetermined way to know ahead of time the characteristics of the gestation period for the program you have in mind.

Effective, no-nonsense planning provides the disciplines and techniques, however, to assess and quantify accurately the time to be alloted to the required events and, finally, the end objective.

Because planning supplies useful, relevant, and measurable progress reports to monitor performance, the effective manager can confidently initiate several plans simultaneously. A professionally prepared plan and valid, timely reporting enable the effective manager to ensure that he is optimally conserving time in each of the ongoing programs.

Planning is the only technique available to an effective manager for ensuring that his organizational efforts have latched onto the endless belt of time. He can be assured that performance and results will be better next month or next year than they were last month or last year. He can measure progress—as time goes by. (Time really doesn't go by, you know. It is, more precisely, *we* who go by). He will be confident that time is on "his side."

PRINCIPLE 16

Planning Makes You Effective—Which Is Better than Merely Efficient

"Effective" means to do the "right thing" at the "right time." "Efficient" means only to do something in a "better" way. "Effective" connotes the notions of change and of objectives that are sought. "Efficient" connotes "tuck-pointing," an improvement to an already existing program or effort. The department foreman is traditionally responsible for achieving labor efficiency variance goals. The Vice President Operations or maybe even the President is (or should be) responsible for labor effectiveness.

"Effective" is a line, rather than staff, activity or aspiration. It is in line posts that things happen. More accurately, the line is where things are made to happen. Staff positions are filled by the "Monday morning quarterbacks" of the world, who, *after* the results are posted, enlighten us all on the degree of efficiency with which the results were achieved.

One of the consequences of this effective/efficient distinction is the realization that planning is primarily and naturally a line—rather than staff—function. It is with planning that things are made to happen more effectively.

The disciplines, procedures, and algorithms of planning make it easier, though admittedly more tedious, for a line manager to make sure that the "right thing" is, in fact, done at the "right time."

How poorly or well that "thing" is done is a question of efficiency, of execution. If, for example, a firm is losing money, it is far more important to do the "right thing" of stopping the losses than it is, say, to publish monthly statements more efficiently, that is, two days earlier. The "effective" goal is to stop the losses—to regain profitability. The "efficient" goal of more accurate or earlier reporting of the firm's losses really has little glory, and even less return to the shareholders.

PRINCIPLE 17

Plans Identify Events; People Make Them Happen

The plan documents have been completed. Events have been identified and quantified. Contingency or "fallback" plans have been formalized. The procedures to monitor progress toward those event/objectives have been documented. The relevance and materiality of the measurement yardsticks have been verified. The incremental execution steps are sufficiently small so that gross unfavorable surprises can be avoided. And the plan has been approved! But now what?!

No matter how thoroughly and professionally the plan has been prepared, it will not by itself blossom into fruition. It takes *people* to make the plan come alive. It takes *people* to perform the tasks in such a manner that the planned events do indeed occur on time and in the correct sequence. It takes people to *execute* the plan.

Too much emphasis is placed on the need to motivate those people on whom the fate of the plan rests. Too much emphasis is placed on the need to improve morale. The basic fallacy common to both of these misplaced priorities is that both motivation and morale are end products. They are the result, not the cause, of confidence of performance.

Confidence of performance results, in turn, directly from self-perception of competence. The validity of that self-perception is based on cumulative prior training and experience. Therefore, *before* submittal of the plan for approval, develop an organization plan that demonstrates that the organization *is* sufficiently trained and experienced; it is up to the task. Once that's done, morale and motivation pretty much take care of themselves.

PRINCIPLE 18

Decide to Plan—Because the Plan Is the Decision

There is far too much confusion in managerial ranks about what a decision is and who makes decisions. Let there be no doubt that decisions *will* be made nonetheless! The confusion stems from failing to distinguish a "decision" from "approval (or disapproval) to implement the decision." Let's clarify the distinction. Webster says that a decision is "a conclusion arrived at after consideration." For a business organization context, a more useful definition is of decision is "the result of a comparison of a proposed action to a collection of policies, procedures, formulae, regulations, laws and customs." Decision-making, then, is the process of performing the comparison.

To relate this phenomenon specifically to the basic purposes of this book, the "proposed action" is, of course, a plan. A professional, effective presentation of the plan anticipates and accommodates the comparison questions to policies, procedures, and the rest. Thus *the planner is the decision-maker!* Or certainly should be!

The manager (or management group) to whom the plan is presented merely performs the role of granting or withholding approval to implement. How to obtain approval or avoid disapproval is dealt with in detail elsewhere in this book.

Sadly, it is axiomatic that the very people who bemoan their lack of organizational power are the very same people who avoid planning like the plague. They fail to *use* planning, largely because they don't understand that planning is the essence of decision-making and the only reliable, predictable source of organizational power!

PRINCIPLE 19

Planning Is Not Forecasting

A common and too frequently encountered confusion is the failure to distinguish the difference between planning and forecasting. While there are indeed some surface similarities, there are profound and basic differences. One similarity is that both deal with the future. They often differ, however, in both the time period and the purpose of the exercise. Forecasts almost always deal with the fiscal time periods—quarter, half, year, and so on—because they are concerned almost exclusively with financial data. It is common to speak of income statement forecasts, balance sheet forecasts, and so on. Even subsets of those data are forecasted, e.g. accounts receivable, inventory, sales, order intake, and so on.

Plans, on the other hand, appear in a wide array of time periods—very often not determined by an accounting decision as to when an accounting year should begin or end. A new product plan, for instance, deals with design and development gestation periods. Further, the subject matters of plans tend to lie outside of the accounting system, outside of the Chart of Accounts.

A likely source of the confusion is the traditional (and arbitrary) inclusion of plan time periods within the accounting or fiscal time period. Plans make things happen; they make the numbers that describe performance. Forecasting is largely an assessment of the probability or likelihood that a given set of performance numbers will eventuate.

It is axiomatic that the better the plans (i.e., the more professionally prepared) the better the forecast (i.e., the greater the validity and reliability). Forecasts can never improve performance.

Only plans (or lack thereof) can affect performance—for good or ill—because plans directly affect the behavior or the people who act, who perform, who implement. And it is only through the action of people that any performance is registered at all.

A forecast tries to predict the outcome of the sum of the plans that have been initiated. It tries to capture a midstream merging of numerous ongoing activities. The validity and reliability of a forecast increase with the thoroughness of milestones plan reporting.

Planning is *always* a "before-the-fact" activity. Forecasting, by contrast, is at best a "during-the-fact" activity.

PRINCIPLE 20

Plan Organization with Competence Quanta

No plan of any significance can be really complete without an organization plan to identify *who* will implement the plan. Far too often one finds in the business world that plans are thought to comprise only planned performance numbers or results. The underlying reality is, of course, that performance numbers are generated only by people. Merely to write numbers on a piece of paper is an exercise of hope and wish.

When a well-documented "numbers" plan is coupled with an equally well-prepared "people" plan, the likelihood of reaching planned results improves dramatically.

The prime criterion to assess the validity of the organization plan is the comparison of the competence or acknowledged expertise of the key individuals to the entries in the Columns B through U of Figure 2, "Analysis of Changes in Operating Pre-Tax" (see pages 110–11). It is

47

precisely (as you will learn in Part IV) those entries which both quantify and rank in complexity the planned changes in operating performance. Make sure your organization is at least equal to the planned challenges.

Thoughtful analysis of the planned performance changes will produce insights of the required organizational competence to bring about the planned changes successfully. For example, if a significant portion of planned pre-tax is dependent upon capture of cost reduction by means of material substitution, there had better be enough people on hand at the right time and *with the "right" material expertise.* In the absence of explicit assurance, the likelihood of success for the plan must remain dim at best.

If you are planning operational growth, market expansion, cost reduction, improved labor efficiency, new products, and so on, then by definition you are looking for results not heretofore achieved. Thus your organization has not previously performed the planned tasks, or not at the planned levels.

Careful matching of the operational plan key changes with existing and planned organizational competence separates excellent from merely good business planning. Just as you are planning "chunks" of pre-tax changes, so too should the organization be viewed in terms of quanta of capability to perform to desired levels. Rank the planned changes on a scale of 1 to 10 of increasing complexity. Then rank the corresponding competence of your organization, also on a scale of 1 to 10, of increasing competence. When the complexity of a planned change is a 9 and the best that the existing organization can come up with is, say, a 4 or 5, sound the alarm! You must plan to recruit the talent you need. Mismatches the other way are prophecies of unplanned turnover—the overqualified simply won't stay.

PART II

Planning and Organizational Power

A

The Nature of
Organizational Power

Without doubt, the most important characteristic of organizational power is that by itself it is amoral. It is beyond the scope of good-or-bad judgmental analysis. It is exclusively the most effective direct agent of change. While it is universally true that change does not guarantee progress, it is equally axiomatic that progress is impossible without change.

In a business organization financial results are always the end product of actions by people. There is absolutely no basis for expecting favorable changes in financial results without first effecting changes in the actions of people. Finally, the only way that changes can be effected in the actions of people is through the exercise of organizational power.

Organizational power is a multifaceted phenomenon. It defies simple, single-sentence description. The existence of organizational power is omnipresent, but degrees of potency vary both among individuals and at different times for the same individual. On the one hand, it is as ephemeral as fame: It, too, is fleeting. On the other hand, when you feel it exerted upon you, it takes on a tangibility that you can't ignore.

A Personal Matter

It is a personal thing. While it may pervade an organization, it has meaning only on a one-on-one basis. You gain it one at a time but can lose it all at once, throughout the organization. Central to the phenomenon of organizational power is the notion of establishing a "superior–subordinate" relationship—a "pecking order," if you will. If, somehow, you are able to persuade or convince another that he is "accountable" to you or in some way dependent upon you, then you will establish yourself as his superior. Implicit in the concept of organizational power is the freedom to exercise command over another.

Only extremely rarely will you encounter an individual in the business world who, without struggle, will freely grant you authority over him. No one "gives" you authority or power. Your "superiors" *cannot,* and your "subordinates" *will not.* Painfully often we hear that plaintive and futile cry, "Grant me the authority to . . ." Power exists only to the extent that it is exercised. You will obtain it only in the doing. You will exercise it precisely, and only, to the extent that others allow you. It must be extracted from individuals.

In the battle for power a contest of wills ensues, which, once started, cannot be left undecided. The moral depth to which the battle may sink is in inverse proportion to the strength and desperation of the desire to "win." Never start a contest when you are even the least bit unsure of winning. If your goal is to obtain or regain some of the power that is exercised by someone over you—your "superior"—be ever mindful of the advice, "Never wound a king." If you enter this contest, be absolutely sure that you can win, because the penalty for losing is immediate and irreversible. Further, the damage carries into the future as any new prospective employer will discern your prior attempt at a "palace revolt." That's the label of the loser of the battle—make no mistake about it. By the way, the label of a winner is "the new boss."

If your goal is to enlarge your power over someone who already is a "subordinate," victory similarly must be assured. A "loss" to a "subordinate" will send clear and loud signals throughout the communication network that you're weakening, you're no longer "top dog." The smell of blood will permeate, and organizational sharks, who formerly respected your territorial imperatives, will decide their time has come. Your future tenure will have become more prayer than predictable. So no matter in which direction, up or down, you try to enlarge your power sphere, you inescapably engage in a one-on-one contest of wills.

The amateur identifies the "pecking order" with the published organization chart. Anyone who does so is a born "subordinate." Further, anyone who relies on a title or position to exercise organizational power will, sooner rather than later, be the victim of a "palace revolt." Whenever you spot anyone parading the flashing sign that proclaims "I am the Boss," you are looking at a loser! He has lost control not only of his organization but of himself as well.

At best the organization chart displays only the routing for formal "signoff" approval. Even for this purpose the amateur will mistake a formal "signoff" requirement as a display of organizational power, of "decision-making." In reality the decision, of course, will already have been made. The routing of documentation is only a communication technique. The person who initiated the documentation, obtained consensual approval, accommodated the anticipated criticisms, and "sold" the proposal is the person who really exercised organizational power.

Credibility

For better or worse, organizational power is very frequently equated with ability to predict future events or results. The premise seems to be that the one who can reliably predict the future somehow exercises control over the sequence and occurrence of the intervening events, such that the predicted end situation does, in fact, eventuate. The reliability of forecasting is measured by how close the forecast is to the actual results achieved. The measurement is made, usually, in terms of both timing and quantitative performance. The result of that measurement, in turn, is the measure of the credibility extended to the forecaster in the future.

Credibility, the most potent asset upon which one can base organizational power, consists of two distinct but interrelated types. For brevity, they can be described as "numbers" credibility and "people" credibility. "Numbers" credibility is the less important of the two. It relates essentially to the credibility garnered by forecasting financial or operational results reasonably well. The subject matter forecasted is almost exclusively impersonal or non–people-related. It deals with such matters as order intake, sales, profits, cash flow, inventory, receivables, warranty costs, and the like.

By far the more important type is "people"-oriented forecast credibility. The subject matter here deals with such things as analysis of motivation of past personal behavior, evaluation of future behavior or performance, evaluation of responses by competitors to action taken or not taken. There should be no mystery or question of the reason why this type of forecast credibility far outweighs the "numbers" type of forecast credibility. "Numbers" results are, after all, only the consequence of behavior of people. The behavior of people, in effect, predetermines what the "numbers" results will be.

Therefore, one who demonstrates reliability in forecasting people behavior cloaks himself in the aura of being able to control people behavior—in short, to possess organizational power.

The prerequisite to altering organizational behavior is an understanding of the motivations and predispositions of the individuals who constitute the organization. Remember that organizational power is *always* a one-on-one relationship.

The demonstration of "people" forecasting credibility, in turn and implicitly, lends credibility to "numbers" forecasts. As stated earlier, these two types of credibility are interrelated. To be precise, if "numbers" forecasts turn out to be too inaccurate, "people" forecasting credibility will be indelibly tarnished. The basic lesson? First, be especially careful with "people" forecasts. Second, don't let "numbers" forecasts get too far out of line.

Getting Approval of the Plan: A Preview

"Selling" the proposal, program, or project deserves special attention. It will be dealt with in much greater detail in Part VI of this book. Only the cardinal elements are discussed here.

Essentially the process can best be described as preconditioning. In an organizational hierarchy, surprise is anathema. Yet even this rule is qualified by the rule of reasonableness and significance. In other words, small surprises are allowed—and, if favorable, even welcomed. But big surprises, whether favorable or otherwise, are intolerable. Further, a surprise need not deal exclusively with financial or operational performance. Unanticipated personnel decisions or even unanticipated personnel performance evaluations are included in the ambit of "surprise."

The basic reason why surprises are anathema is that they constitute public evidence of not only a breakdown in organizational communication but a failure to exercise organizational control—organizational power. The credibility of the organization head will have become tarnished. Those with whom he formerly had exclusive contact will cast about within the organization to discover a more reliable source, someone who "really" knows what's going on. The "surprised" superior, in short, loses power. A well-orchestrated surprise may, in fact, be enough to unseat him.

Successful preconditioning of individuals in the "sign-off" chain occurs when you act in a manner consistent with the reality that signers-off are loath to make a decision. They want to wait until the situation is "ripe." They want to be assured that a meaningful consensus exists. They must be led step by step, prior to "formal" submittal, to believe that the program submittal will sail through without a hitch. Their motivation is not only a "protect-your-fanny" objective. It is much more than that. It is the acceptance of another reality: that without broad support or, more important, a state of no pronounced opposition, the success of the program is in dire jeopardy.

The most effective technique to accomplish supportive preconditioning is the practice of establishing a "common memory." It capitalizes on a basic psychological principle: What is familiar cannot be a surprise. The exercise of patience is a given. The seed must be planted and carefully nurtured, generally for a considerable time. Usually the larger the program and the greater the agent of change it represents, the longer the conditioning period that is required. The truly skillful exerciser of power will so whet the appetite of the signer-off that we will (even) be directed to present the program formally to the signer-off. As a rule it is couched in such terms as, "You know that problem (opportunity) that we've talked about for (whatever time period). When are you going to do something about it? Why don't you prepare a proposal for my review? I'd like to see your thinking about it."

To Persuade or to Convince?

There are only two techniques to be used for preconditioning. Only seldom is one or the other used exclusively, even when dealing with the same individual. The choices available are first to persuade and second to convince. Persuasion is an appeal to intuition, to emotion, to "gut-feeling," to instinct, and to "heart of hearts." We easily believe what we fear or desire. Persuasion is particularly effective when dealing with sales personnel and entrepreneurs. It is notably ineffective when dealing with controllers, auditors, and treasurer types. The more the person being dealt with is emotionally oriented rather than rationally, the more useful is the persuasion technique. The key to optimal use of these two techniques is to understand, and act upon, the difference between being "logical" and being "right."

The nature of persuasion being what it is, the use of "numbers" or quantitative approaches will be not only unhelpful but probably even counterproductive. To persuade effectively, you will find that use of adverbs and adjectives is most helpful. You want to stir emotions. You want your target to *feel* that failure to support (or to withhold opposition to) your plan will result in disaster. And disaster must be prioritized first in terms of *personal* disaster for the persuadee, then, second, in terms of disaster for the firm.

The consequences of failure to implement the plan are best described in terms of excessive "downside" jeopardy. The glass should be not only half-empty but cracked as well. "If we don't do this now, we won't be able to recoup later." "The potentially adverse developments are *so* severe that reporting it 'upstairs' is a must. And when they begin to interrogate you about it, you'd be a lot better off if you had some recovery program in hand." "Competition is talking about introducing a new (or improved) product, and our board has heard about it. You know they're going to ask you (us) what you're (we're) doing about it. You (we) had better come up with something!" These are only a few variations on the theme. You have heard (even perhaps used) many others over the years.

To convince, on the other hand, one must marshal a quantitative rather than a qualitative argument or presentation. It is an appeal to logic, to reason rather than emotion. If the evidence is compelling, it is possible to obtain acquiescence or at least a muting of disagreement. Conviction generates merely recognition and agreement; only persuasion fathers commitment and dedication. That's why nobody ever has "company loyalty"; they have only "personal loyalty." The "company" is simply too remotely impersonal to forge an emotional link.

The best way to convince is to follow this simple pattern: First, gather enough raw data to establish credibility for the basis of your presentation. Some selectivity of data collection is okay, provided you don't go too far, and provided your target is highly unlikely to have a better data base than the one you have. Generally, physical data have more impact than accounting system data. To dramatize a decline in sales, units shipped will enhance conviction more than (only) dollars. Or else, restate sales dollars to remove the effect of inflation, especially if prices have risen significantly.

Second, based on that raw data, draw operational and financial inferences to measure the disastrous consequences that will ensue if action is not taken. Extrapolate expense and cost run-rates. Evaluate the financial follow-on consequences of lowered gross margin content of decreased order intake levels. Don't forget the unabsorbed burden penalties. Numerically, infer the operational and financial consequences of the worsening gap between plant operational levels and practical capacity.

Third, rank the inferences by probability of occurrence of impact. The most useful ranking method is evaluation of the combined effect of frequency and severity. These are the same analytical tools used in industrial accident or plant safety programs. In development of conviction, however, you are dealing with the future rather than the past. So while "frequency" is conjectural, it is based on the inferences drawn from the raw data. The likelihood of occurrence is essentially a "given." The only point at issue is the duration of the condition. Therefore, the development of several scenarios will make your presentation more convincing. Only three scenarios need be presented: "Worst Case," "Probable," and "Best Case." Carefully define the underlying assumptions used for each of the three. The "Worst Case" is, of course, the most conservative.

The "severity" of the inferences should also be included in the scenarios. "Severity" issues deal with the number of dollars involved with each of the inferences.

The fourth and final step is to draw the conclusions. And the conclusions—no surprise—just happen to be the elements and components of your plan. The scenario most likely to be most readily accepted or at least unopposed is the "Worst Case." The "Worst Case" scenario, if properly drawn, depicts the least improvement in an unfavorable condition or the least additional gain in a favorable condition.

Steps 1, 2, and 3 present a quantitative description of the problem(s). Step 4 presents quantitative solutions based upon changes in operating circumstances. These changes always affect organizations—reductions, additions, and/or changes in assignment. To the extent that your conclusions are implemented, you will have exercised organizational power!

Finally, don't overlook the possibility of using the conviction technique as preliminary to the more powerful persuasion technique. There will be times when the conviction technique can be used as a two-by-four across the bridge of the nose—it'll get their attention! Once you've got it, you are in a much better position to persuade them! But much more on this later.

"Up-Power" and "Down-Power"

There are only two directions in which organizational power can be exercised. One can attempt to control either one's "superiors" or one's "subordinates." First, let's explore control of one's "superiors." For convenience, let's call it "up-power."

The most important realization is that all you want them to do is—*nothing*. You only really need for them to do nothing at all as you attempt to broaden your sphere of power. Oh, sure, it's great if they give you public support and encouragement, but it's really not necessary at all. For you to be successful, all you need to avoid is a veto. The exercise of "veto power" is the second most powerful weapon that a "superior" can bring to bear. No, the most powerful is *not* termination—it is indifference, nonrecognition, a version of being placed "in Coventry." It renders you impotent, because if you are known to not have the superior's ear, only the most unsophisticated (and unuseful) members of the organization will acknowledge your existence. The signal is usually a transfer from a line to a staff or consultant job. You can ordinarily escape indifference by use of conviction rather than persuasion.

It is required, to exercise "up-power," that the superior perceive you to be interested in making his life easier. This interest ranges all the way from running your group so well that it never presents problems for him to supporting him in his personal relations and problems.

Persuasion is the better technique to obtain entree to his private, personal world. It is useful to do so because of the need to break down his "aloofness barrier." Absent a degree of aloofness, it is impossible to exercise organizational power. He will try to keep the barrier in place and even to heighten it. To the extent that you allow him to do that, you will fail to achieve organizational power.

Another way to break down the "aloofness barrier" is to press the "superior's" hot buttons. Everyone of us has special interests, predispositions, even prejudices. It just makes plain common sense that you will never influence anyone if all you talk about is subjects in which they have little or no interest. To achieve organizational power, it is necessary first to consciously and purposefully seek out the hot buttons and second (merely) to press them—as often and as hard as you can.

The old cliché of "making the boss look good" will forever apply. There are many ways to do it. They range all the way from helping him to achieve the superficial improvement of his physical appearance to the substantive achievement of results that are always "better than" budget, forecast, or whatever. And therein lies the rub, eh? How in the world does one *always* obtain "better than" results? Well, it's time to face up to a key prerequisite of exerting organizational power. Absent a unique and inviolable personal tie, the only people who can exercise power are, indeed, the powerful! *You have to be good, really good at your job!*

In fact, the better you are at your job, the less important it is to rely on the persuasion technique. If you're not really all that good, and therefore must rely excessively on persuasion, there is only one caveat I leave with you: "Time wounds all heels!" All "politicians" rely on persuasion, but not all who use persuasion are "politicians!"

A time-proven technique to obtain "better than" results is simply to "lowball" the yardstick. The annual budget preparation is the occasion for a "joust" between superior and subordinate, as we shall explore in Part IV. The superior, if he's any good at all, wants you to commit to higher levels of performance. You, of course, would really like to establish a lower goal. The opponents enter the meeting room and the game begins. Thrust and parry. Exogenous variables, indigenous variables; controllables, uncontrollables; too many people, not enough people; rate of inflation is going up, rate of inflation is going down; and on and on.

To win the battle you must be prepared with both persuasion and conviction weapons. The well-prepared superior has both at his disposal; the subordinate has only conviction. Except for some remarkable coincidence, or unless careful identification of the superior's hot buttons has been made beforehand, a subordinate's gut-feeling is never a match for a superior's gut-feeling, and certainly never a match for a superior's conviction! On the other hand, a subordinate's quantitative argument can overcome a superior's conviction. And it *can* penetrate a persuasion: Nothing is so devastating to an opinion as a number.

While it's important to obtain "better than" results, it is equally important—perhaps even more important in certain situations—to be perceived as the dispenser of "good news." Once you have that reputation, no door remains unopened, no phone call remains unanswered. Your presence is first welcome, then sought. Your counsel will be solicited. You will be exercising organizational power. You are a "comer," a "winner."

With all this publicity and recognition, avoid as best you can the superior's perception of you as a threat. An organizational "hot dog" has *no* organizational future: The more successful you are in gaining "up-power" the more difficult the future will be. It is almost invariably the case that eventually you *will* be perceived as a threat. One of the best defenses against the day of reckoning is the consolidated support of subordinates. Do *not* attempt to exercise "up-power" until you have maximized exercise of "down-power."

There are two remaining points to make with regard to exercise of "up-power." Both of them relate directly to plans and planning. First, preempt winning positions. Sure, easy to say; how do you do it? A winning position is one that is virtually assured of not only the superior's indifference but positive approval as well. At the highest management levels this means knowing what the owners *really* want done with this business. Identifying the winning position is closely akin to identifying hot buttons. Discern what they really want done, then formulate the plans to accomplish it. Like General Grant, be there "firstest with the mostest." Claim the high ground as yours by being the author of the plan by which the result can be achieved.

Plan = Knowledge = Power

A plan is knowledge, and as such it possesses inherent power. Develop a plan sufficiently detailed such that it demands that you become knowledgeable in depth. The "Summary and Conclusions" section is probably all that your superiors will really read. Your personal presentation, selectively seasoned with persuasion and conviction, will provide implicit reassurance that a detailed reading is uncalled for. Once you get the plan in motion, you are the possessor of in-progress knowledge. That makes you the possessor of latent power. They must come to you for information, for prospects, for status, and for prognosis.

Divulge the information selectively, and you will exercise power thereby. A particularly bothersome subordinate can be dispatched, with appropriate concern and regret, if you control the flow of communication that explains why a particularly critical date was missed or an important task was unfinished.

Let me make something "perfectly clear." The purpose of this book is to explain *how* effectively to gain organizational power. It is not my purpose to exhort you to use that power in any particular way. The aim of this book is not to preach moralistically. It is, rather, to make you aware and knowledgeable about the tools and tactics that can be used by you or against you. By themselves these tools and tactics are amoral. The ends you seek in the exercise of power are for you alone to determine. Careless use of these tools and techniques may be dangerous to the health of your business career. This book can arm you with an array of weapons that are always usable and always effective. Once learned and put into practice, they will consistently overpower the many superficial, Machiavellian techniques that the amateurs foolishly continue to employ. No-Nonsense Planning makes mincemeat of manipulative machinations.

So before you begin to apply No-Nonsense Planning, be absolutely sure that you know, in your heart of hearts, to which ends and in what manner you will exercise power. No-Nonsense Planning will enable you to acquire the power, but only you know what you shall do with it. Honesty is probably the best policy after all—it has *so* little competition! My earlier book, *No-Nonsense Management,* shows you how to use organizational power most effectively and productively.

Keeping your record strong is certainly at least as important as gaining visibility with the "king-makers." Your batting average is influenced not alone by the number of times you are identified with plans. The importance of the plan adds a weighting factor. Think in terms of the "frequency/severity" measures used for industrial personal injury accidents.

One plan that successfully opens new profitable, growing, and major markets to the firm counts more than almost any number of plans that marginally reduce, say, travel expenses. The basic principles are these: The greater the risk, the greater the reward; the greater the "bottom line" impact, the greater the impact on batting average.

Having said all that, your judgment of the likelihood of success of the plan is critical, because your decision to become identified with it will directly affect your batting record. Knowing when to avoid accountability is a skill first to be acknowledged and then to be finely honed.

Excessive avoidance of accountability, meaning consistent avoidance of *personal* responsibility, can never really improve your batting record. At the very best it only reduces the number of times at bat. It tends to preserve a batting record rather than improve it. Conversely, excessive embracing of accountability will certainly lead to more strikeouts than necessary. In short, you've got to learn when to hold 'em and when to fold 'em.

Avoiding a "Veto"

The need to avoid a superior's veto was mentioned briefly earlier. Let us take a minute to explore that requirement. Avoidance of a veto is essential principally because a veto signals the organization that you are ignorant of even the mechanics, to say nothing of the subtleties, of organizational power. A veto is a public announcement that your ego exceeded your managerial judgment. Not only is receiving a veto a stupid blunder, it is, tragically, totally unnecessary. During the preconditioning process, there will be, to the discerning eye and ear, a more than adequate array of signals to tell you that you are pursuing the wrong course—pressing the wrong buttons.

The most frequent error precipitating a veto is improper timing. Your rush to gain visibility is premature. The issue was not yet ripe. You probably waited a "normal" length of time to let your superiors get used to your proposal, forgetting that there is no fixed or even predictable gestation period for an idea. Lack of understanding of that reality is the direct cause of suffering a veto because of your premature pressure for a "decision."

The Carrot and the Stick

The exercise of "down-power" includes those personnel who are already "subordinates" on the organization chart. To the professional exerciser of organization power, however, organization chart "peers" are also "down" targets. The roles are, not surprisingly, reversed from those dealing with "up-power." The "down-power" targets will attempt to deal with you as you would when dealing with a "superior." The exercise of "down-power," then, comprises those actions which an effective superior would take.

The keystone upon which all else is based is your subordinates' perception of you as a dispenser of both rewards and punishment. If they fail so to perceive you, you will not be acknowledged as a "superior." It's as simple as that. The objective, then, is to present yourself in such a way that their view of you as the authoritative source of rewards and punishment is vibrant and real.

Rewards come in a wide variety. They range from the immediately tangible (money) through those that lead to tangible rewards (promotions or title changes) to the subtle psychic income of "recognition" (an award, a public tribute). The choice of reward, to be effective, will be carefully tailored to the individual's "hot button." Yes, subordinates also have hot buttons. Recall that organizational power is exercised on a one-to-one basis, so the degree to which you know the individual you are dealing with will measure the effectiveness with which you select the reward carrot.

A note of caution with regard to dispensing rewards. Do not grant them in such profusion that you either strengthen an individual's power base too much or preclude any disciplinary action on your part against him later. In other words, do not reward to the point where he no longer feels genuinely vulnerable. It is impossible to exercise power over anyone who does not feel vulnerable, whether he really is or not.

Vulnerability itself requires some discussion. In a business organization context, the meaning of vulnerability has to do with the notions of being open to criticism, to loss of face, to attack on one's credibility. With only rare exceptions, vulnerability arises from "numbers" discrepancies and leads to judgment challenge of the person's "people" decisions. To illustrate, when an individual fails to meet a scheduled date, he has committed a "numbers" discrepancy. Absent some compelling reason for the failure, that individual has opened himself up to attack (i.e., become vulnerable) with the more devastating criticism of lack of judgment, lack of maturity (most often phrased as "not enough grey hairs"), or lack of organizational control.

There are three sure steps for establishing the vulnerability of a "subordinate." To be effective, they must be taken in the given sequence. The first step is to make them "accountable" for something. If persons are not held accountable for anything, they are impervious to attack—they are invulnerable. Accountability is based on the existence of a prior assignment. There is nothing to be accountable for if there is no obligation to perform, and there can be no obligation to perform if there has been no assignment, no formalization of the obligation.

Once accountability has been established by a measurable assignment, the second step is to enforce the obligation to "explain." When the obligation exists to "explain"— results, performance, and so on—the superior–subordinate bond is established. *The subordinate must recognize the obligation to explain that for which he is accountable.*

If the assignment, from which accountability rises, is phrased in vague or general terms, the burden of explanation is trivially easy to carry. In general the degree to which the assignment is phrased specifically determines how effectively it will establish vulnerability of the assignee. Further, the greater the number of accountabilities, the greater the resultant vulnerability of the assignee.

In short, greater vulnerability of the assignee will occur to the extent that the assignment is expressed both specifically and in a larger number of performance measures rather than fewer. The intensity of vulnerability increases, as noted earlier, from "numbers" vulnerability to "people" vulnerability. The surest way to establish vulnerability in another is to proceed in the same sequence. Thus, the *assignment-accountability-explanation procedure will lay the groundwork for "numbers" vulnerability.* Depending upon the subordinate's performance, he may or may not expose himself to the more important "people" vulnerability. The fact alone that jeopardy exists means that vulnerability exists.

"Numbers" discrepancies occur every day. Usually they are not severe enough to cause serious damage, but when issues regarding judgment or emotional maturity are raised, the barriers to promotion to higher levels have become all but insurmountable for that individual.

Just as rewards vary in form and shape, so do punishments. They range all the way from a mild rebuke administered privately while walking along a hallway or in an elevator through a memo with "suggestions" for improvement, a critical performance appraisal for the personnel file, and demotion, to termination. Without question, however, the most severe punishment, as mentioned earlier, is to paint the individual as organizationally impotent, devoid of power or influence. At least it's the most severe form of punishment used against an individual who aspires to exercise power. It all depends, of course, on the *individual* involved. Rather than a punishment, such a reputation just might make him the happiest person in the group, in which case you would have granted a reward! Not all individuals seek to exercise power; they shun the responsibility they feel is attendant on being a "boss."

Termination is the final punishment. It should be handled carefully. It will affect the entire organization—for good or ill. It will reflect on you—for good or ill. The reaction of the organization is a meaningful indicator of the professionalism with which the termination was handled. You know you really fouled it up if the reaction is "Oh, my God!" That tells you that you are in for rough times ahead. You have surprised the organization; you are now vulnerable to attacks on *your* judgment, emotional maturity, and so on.

But if the reaction is "ho-hum," you know you handled it well. The group was thoroughly preconditioned. And if the "ho-hum" is followed by "What took you so long?" you can even claim the high ground of having too much human compassion. You're a bloody hero!

Unlike dealing with a "superior," whom you want to do nothing, you do indeed want a subordinate to do "something." Namely, you want him to do what you want him to do. Your performance record is the sum of the performance records of your subordinates. So the more they do, the better your performance record. Someone once said, "Management is the art of getting work done through others." You cannot be a manager if you are not a "superior." You get them to do something by selective use of carrots and sticks.

Just as you sought, in exercising "up-power," to break down the aloofness barrier of your superior, it is equally important to keep your aloofness barrier up when dealing with subordinates. The easiest method to ensure retention of aloofness is to ensure, early on, the vulnerability of your subordinates. The relationship can be expressed: The need to establish the aloofness barrier is inversely proportional to the vulnerability of the subordinate.

Finally, exercise your veto power with care. Use it

sparingly. The impact of a veto is diminished by the frequency of its use. When you do use the veto, it should hit the organization with impact. Too frequent use of the veto is self-defeating. The impact on the organization will fade. Too frequent use of any single technique will yield progressively less effective results. No surprise. Don't ignore this important psychological principle of diminishing response to a constant stimulus.

B

The Eight Ways in Which Planning Enhances Organizational Power

The planning process offers direct and effective assistance to the establishment and enhancement of organizational power. It matters not whether you are trying to exercise "up-power" or "down-power." In fact, failure to exploit the potential of planning will certainly diminish your power prospects and may even preclude your success.

First, how does the preparation of well-thought-out plans to which superiors have been preconditioned enhance up-power prospects? There are at least eight ways. All eight will be discussed, not necessarily in any particular rank order. As the presentor, you will have preempted the "winning" position. You know that your plan will be well received and that it deals with objectives held dear by superiors. You will have pressed their hot buttons.

Because the "approvers" were preconditioned, they will do "nothing," except approve your plan. Which is precisely what you want them to do.

Your "boss" will look good. One of *his* group will be viewed as in control of events. Because of the careful and thorough preconditioning, his veto will have been successfully avoided. Because it's *your* plan, progress reporting falls to you. In other words, *you* control the flow of information.

Now come the really tough points. Once your plan is approved, you have the task of reaching performance levels "better than" the plan. Largely you must rely and depend on *your* subordinates to deliver the results. To be viewed as a dispenser of "good news," you must first have "good news" to dispense. Therefore, the manner in which you exercise "down-power" is critical.

Remember that *you* want subordinates to do "something." The plan you presented contains numerous quantitative, impersonally measured milestones. Because your plan was constructed in that manner, you are in a position to pursue the assignment-accountability-explanation sequence with subordinates. In short, you are now able to utilize their vulnerability to obtain "better than" plan results. Your aloofness barriers should be intact. Should all else fail, or should one subordinate or another show unusually challenging tendencies, there is always your veto to rely on.

The plan itself forces "explanation" from subordinates. No matter how detailed or comprehensive the plan is, there will always be variances from plan. It is precisely these variances or differences from planned performance that require explanation. Further, results never exceed *all* of the plan goals, objectives, or milestones. As the reviewer of results compared to the plan, you can, at virtually any time, transmit upstream objective and impersonal evaluations to "make" or "break" the doer—in short, you exercise power!

The value of planning quantitative, measurable performance milestones cannot be overemphasized. If only prose explanations are required, the articulate escape accountability. "Gut-feeling" gains credibility. Only a "numbers" explanation precludes escape from vulnerability by subordinates.

The purpose of this section was to acquaint you with the "why" of planning from a personal standpoint. There is simply no point in providing you with the "nuts and bolts" of plan preparation without making you aware of some of the "real world" implications and consequences of planning. You can gain a reputation for functional excellence without planning, but you can't exercise organizational power without planning! You can be known as a truly fine controller or "operations guy" or salesman without ever developing a plan. If that's the extent of your ambition, read no further! Put this book down and go back to your debits and credits, your material discrepancies, or your call report. But if you aspire to top management, then read on. Let's proceed from the "Why" to the "How To."

PART III

How to Plan a Business Start-Up: Just Thirty-Nine Steps to Success!

A

Planning Procedure
Overview

Before we begin our journey through Figure 1, let me
"map" the area for you. There are thirty-nine steps. They
fall into only five categories, as follows:

1. Documenting a Plan

There are five such steps. The output of these steps is
essentially the same: a package of traditional plan documents with milestones, maybe a PERT chart, maybe a
Critical Path format, supporting and explanatory prose,
assumptions, premises, mission statements, tables of organization, financial projections, and so on and so on. In
short, its the "usual" stuff that is so often the focus of
seminars, books, and so forth. You cannot have gone
at all far in management if you have never completed
or participated in completing a "business plan" or "profit
plan."

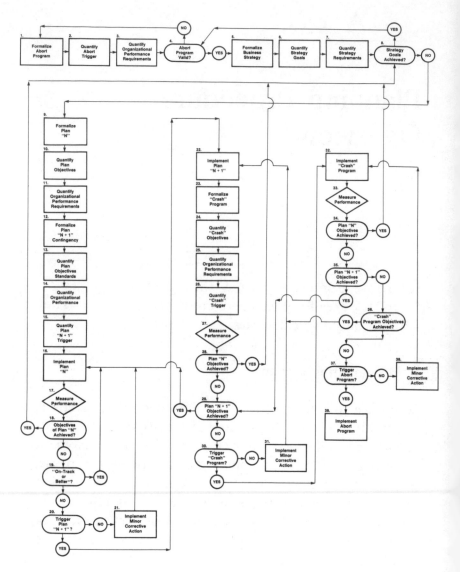

Figure 1. Steps in Planning Procedure

82

2. Quantification

There are twelve quantification steps. About 31 percent of the activity revolves around affixing numbers to events. The primary purposes of this activity are first to anticipate circumstances or conditions that, if realized, will cause certain predetermined actions to be taken or not taken. Second, extensive quantification provides the basis for virtual elimination of subjective, emotional (rather than rational) decision-making. The idea is to depersonalize the process, to operate and make decisions objectively. Third, quantification provides the basis for organizational control and, consequently, management control of the entire process.

3. Question-Asking

There are also twelve steps that ask questions. The questions are always posed as comparisions. The comparisions are also always the same: Measured actual performance is compared to predetermined quantitative criteria or yardsticks.

4. Action Implementation

These seven steps are what most management amateurs call "the work" when they complain that planning takes too much time away from getting on with "the work." These are the day-to-day "operating the business" steps.

5. Performance Measurement

These three steps provide the answers to the questions at various stages. To perform these steps at all one must make absolutely sure that two conditions have been met. First, the planned action must be described in measurable terms, whether obtained from the physical world, from the accounting system world, or from a combination of both. Second, the procedures must be thought out beforehand and put in place to ensure accurate and timely collection of the data, so that the comparisons to actual performance can be made and, in turn, the posed questions can be validly answered, so that the action taken based on those answers will be effective, relevant, and material. Let's recap:

	Number of Steps	Percentage of Total Steps
1. Documenting a Plan	5	12
2. Quantification	12	31
3. Question-Asking	12	31
4. Action Implementation	7	18
5. Performance Measurement	3	8

A few key inferences can be made from a study of that recap. First, more than two-thirds of all of the steps consist of quantification, question-asking and performance measurement. These three activities are the stuff of which organizational power is made. In contrast, only 18 percent of the steps consists of "doing the work," or action implementation. In short, the one who performs the quantification, the performance measurement, and the question-asking is the one who exercises the power.

Now let us briefly review the major modules or subroutines of Figure 1. Again, there are only five. They are grouped as follows:

Module	Steps
I	1 through 4
II	5 through 8
III	9 through 21
IV	22 through 31
V	32 through 38

MODULE I: Steps 1 Through 4

The purpose of this module is to tell us when and how we abort the business venture if actual operating results are so poor as to activate the Abort Trigger.

MODULE II: Steps 5 Through 8

The function of this module is to document and quantify our business strategies. Here we carefully define what business we're really getting into. We quantify the goals we seek and measure the time frame in which we seek to achieve them.

MODULE III: Steps 9 Through 21

There are three purposes with which this module deals. (1) The initial operating plan is documented and quantified. (2) We formalize our first contingency plan ("fallback" plan or "recoup" plan) so that, if actual performance warrants, we can minimize further adverse effects by having our contingency plan ready to implement. (3) We begin implementation of our initial operating plan. We hope, of course, that execution of our initial operating plan will result in achievement of our strategy goals.

MODULE IV: Steps 22 Through 31

The purposes of this module parallel those in Module III. The difference is that operating results of our initial operating plan were unacceptable. Thus the first purpose of this module is to implement our contingency plan. But, following the pattern in Module III, we recognize Murphy's Law and anticipate even further failure to perform to plan by formalizing a "Crash" Program. The idea is to implement the Crash Program only if, after repeated corrective actions, performance fails even to reach Contingency Plan levels.

MODULE V: Steps 32 Through 39

The pattern of this module is not dissimilar to the two earlier. We get to this module only if actual operating performance fails to achieve Contingency Plan levels. The first thing we do is implement the Crash Program. Our business is in deep trouble. We keep monitoring performance and taking further minor corrective action until, alas, the Abort Trigger is activated, and, in Step 39, we implement the Abort Program that we documented in Module I.

This part, Part III, is the first of three "cookbook" segments, which present planning formats for the most important planning functions in a for-profit business. In this part we deal with where it all begins. We face the question, "Should we go into (this or that) business?" And if we should go into the business, "What kind of controls should we put in place to make sure that, if the business fails to meet our goals, we don't throw good money after bad?" While the details of year-to-year planning for an ongoing business are presented in the Part IV, the proper time to understand, establish, and commit to the overall planning concepts to control the ongoing firm is precisely at the time of its inception.

All of the discussion in this part is summarized in Figure 1. It is organized as a flow chart so that the steps *and* the sequence of those steps can be quickly grasped. The flow chart format is especially useful too because the planning (and control) process is an iterative process. That is, feedback of real-world actual results may trigger alternative courses of action. The following discussion traces the numbered steps in Figure 1.

B

Detailed Planning Steps

1. *Formalize Abort Programs*

The first step is the most critical and usually the most overlooked by managements who try to start a new business. Anticipate that the business will fail, then decide *how* you will get out. Is it the kind of business where you can simply close the doors? Or will you wind up with receivables, inventory, fixed assets, warranty and parts supply obligations, and so on? You should have a fairly good idea of the number of dollars that will be tied up in various areas. You will also have a good idea of the extent of contractual obligations you will have incurred, especially if you established distributor relationships.

The output of this step should be a thought-out program of how you will handle winding up. Certainly the first alternative to consider is sale of the business. Obtain financial and legal counsel to provide realistic appraisal of the benefits, advantages, disadvantages, and limitations of the various alternatives.

2. *Quantify Abort Trigger*

The purpose of this step is to identify the circumstances in which the business will be terminated. All too often in business, good money is thrown after bad because of emotional and ego involvement. To the extent that quantitative criteria are identified in this step, the decision to continue with the business is depersonalized. Consequently, cutting losses can more effectively be done by avoidance of useless subjective debate.

Probably the most useful measure, among many others, is "gross margin content in the forward-aged order backlog." In other words, you decide: "If gross margin content in the forward-aged order backlog falls below N dollars, we get out of the business."

Cash flow, of course, is another critical measure. Realized price is yet another criterion that gives insight into the gross margin content criterion mentioned earlier. If gross margin content is unsatisfactory because of failure to obtain planned prices due to a misreading of either competitive action or the market generally, it is a more severe condition than that of unsatisfactory gross margin because of excessive production costs. One cannot control action by the competition or buying decisions in the market generally. One can, however, exercise some remedial control over costs.

There is no universally applicable set of criteria. Selection will depend upon the specific conditions and circumstances prevalent at the time. The important point, however, is to recognize that the very first step to take is to determine under what conditions you will abandon or otherwise *get out* of the business that you're considering getting into.

3. *Quantify Organizational Performance Requirements*

Merely putting together the financial package is not enough to give assurance of successful actual performance. Projected performance can become reality only through the action of an organization. It is, after all, people who perform the tasks. And it has long been established that personal accountability enhances the likelihood of success. So the output of this step is to express the abort program objectives in terms of the individuals whose collective activity generate the actual results. Not only are monitoring and control thereby enhanced, but these personal performance standards can also be used as the basis for an incentive compensation program.

This planning step can be as difficult as, or even more difficult than, quantification of the preceding step. Quantifying the tasks and subtasks individual by individual requires considerable strength of forethought. But rest assured that even if this step is completed with no more than 90 or 95 percent effectiveness, the outcome will be dramatically more favorable than if this step had not been performed at all.

If this step is reasonably well done, losses will be cut

significantly. And cutting losses to a minimum is *the* ultimate goal of an abort decision.

4. *Is the Abort Program Valid?*

This is a sanity-check question. Before going farther, compare the abort program with the abort test criteria to make sure they are consistent and complementary. As you developed the program, you may have gained new insight into the criteria that may affect the get-out decision. You will see later how and when we return to this question during the iterative process.

5. *Formalize Strategy*

Depending, of course, on the type and size of business that you are considering launching, there should be strategies, rather broadly stated, to guide and delimit the tactical, day-to-day activities. The output of this step should be series of essentially prose statements to explain, generally, how you will proceed to achieve what you want to achieve.

Should sales be made through direct salesmen or distributors? Shall we be a "full-line" house, or shall we specialize in only a few lines? Will we do any fabrication, assembly, or testing? Should we be pioneers or me-tooers? Shall we be known as a top-of-the-line, high-quality firm? Or will we be medium-grade? Will profits come more from volume than from margin, or vice versa? These questions give only a taste of the number and types of questions that need to be not only asked but answered as well.

6. *Quantify Strategy Goals*

After having thoroughly examined the basic strategy element, the output of this step is to quantify those strategy statements. If we're going to sell through direct salesmen, how many will we have? Over what time period? How, and how much, will we pay them? When will training be complete? In other words, for every strategy statement, assign a number of some related kind. If a manufacturing plant is needed, ennumerate the equipment, identify the square footage requirement, and so on.

7. *Quantify Strategy Requirements*

The purpose of this step is to document the requirements, as specifically as possible, needed to attain the strategy goals. The principal requirement is cash. How much, when, and from where are the key questions. If plant is needed, how will it be obtained? New construction? Rehabilitation of a used plant? Expansion of existing plant?

Is the organization in place? If not, what will it take to get it there? Where are the principal "gaps"? What is required to fill them with the quantity and quality of personnel required?

8. *Strategy Goals Achieved?*

This is the second sanity-test question. What you want to do here is double-check that, as you developed quantitative requirements, you supported and met the goals you established earlier.

In subsequent iterations, when you are led to this step again, the question will be whether real-world actual results have occurred such that the strategy goals have been achieved. We shall discuss that point later as we discuss Steps 13, 20, 25, and 30.

9. *Formalize Plan "N"*

The output of this step is the initial operational plan, full-blown with sales, engineering, operations, marketing, and finance plans, for the first year of our new business. The documents prepared in this step will strongly resemble those prepared in Step 4. They are essentially prose expressions of the nature and type of action that we plan to occur in the coming period. They should be consistent with and supportive of the strategy formalization in Step 4.

10. *Quantify Plan Objectives*

Once the basic plans have been put into words, with mission statements and tactical detail, the purpose of this step is to translate that prose into quantitative performance objectives.

What we're dealing with here are the traditional monthly cash flow, income, and balance sheet statements, supported by order intake, product cost, and other projections. The output of this step is the familiar "numbers" package.

11. *Quantify Organizational Performance Requirements*

Because this is *the* plan used to launch the business, and because organizational performance in the first year of operation is *so* critical to avoidance of abort conditions, this step should be performed with the utmost care and detail.

This is the set of documents you will use to maintain management control of the organization and the business. Be somewhat generous with incentive compensation payments for performance better than plan. The likelihood of staying in business for years is strongly enhanced by performance in excess of the first year's objectives.

Okay, we've finished Steps 8, 9, and 10. By God, but we've got this thing figured out. We know who is supposed to do what and we've got numbers to track progress. Let's launch, shall we? *NOPE.* Not yet. Rather, let's *anticipate:* Suppose there are major shortfalls from the plan, what will we do then? Rather than just "wing it" if we get to that point, let's put a contingency plan together.

12. *Formalize Plan "N + 1" Contingency*

13. *Quantify Objectives*

14. *Quantify Organizational Performance Standards*

15. *Quantify Plan "N + 1" Trigger*

These four steps are discussed together because they are similar in approach, content, and output to Steps 9, 10, and 11. The only difference is Step 15. In this step the task is to predetermine the performance circumstances in which the contingency plan will be launched. It is similar in concept to Step 1. In Step 15 what we're after is a quantitative measure of what constitutes a "major unfavorable deviation" from projected performance.

Steps 12, 13, and 14 are the familiar PNP (prose-numbers-people) pattern, but this time we're looking at the business at a time when actual performance has been disappointing by more than a little. But the pattern remains the same. Once again, before beginning the business we prethink our way out of anticipated developments.

After quantifying the "trigger," the contingency plan is first prepared in prose, then translated into numbers, and finally the new numbers are related to organization.

Because in the iterative process we may find it necessary to develop several, successive corrective plans, the notation "N + 1" is used. Since the initial plan is the "N" Plan, the first corrective plan or modification is called "N + 1". If the "N + 1" Plan is launched, it in effect replaces the "N" Plan. If a second modification plan is needed, it becomes the "N + 2" Plan, and so on.

Of special note: Don't implement the first plan until you have thoroughly documented the "fallback" or "recoup" plan.

16. *Implement Plan "N"*

At last we are ready to begin the action! Initiating commitment of dollars and other resources any earlier simply must end in failure—or at best minimal and certainly suboptimal results. The materials are purchased, the people are hired, the promotion programs are formalized, the plan is made operational. The tussle and tumble of business begins.

17. *Measure Performance*

As the activity grows and days go by, the need for careful and useful measurement multiplies. "Actual-to-plan" comparisons are the order of the day. With organizational performance requirements having been previously reduced to numbers, tracking results to individuals is greatly facilitated. Individuals can be called to account. Gross failure surprises will have been precluded. All this preparatory work to measure performance easily, accurately, *and* objectively merely sets the stage for the next critical step.

18. *Objectives of Plan "N" Achieved?*

The answer sought is binary—either the Plan "N" objectives were achieved or not. The comparison is impersonal, quantitative, and objective. A disarmingly simple, but absolutely crucial, question.

If the answer is YES, we return to Step 8 to determine whether our strategy goals have also been achieved. If not, we go back to further and continuing implementation of Plan "N." If the answer is NO, we proceed to the next question-step.

19. *Is Performance "On-Track or Better"?*

The purpose of this step is to determine whether we're doing okay even though the original objectives have not yet been achieved. If we *are* on-track or better, then we merely return to Step 16 and continue implementation of Plan "N."

20. *Trigger Plan "N + 1"?*

If the results of Step 19 disclose that we are *not* on-track or better, we test in this next step whether the actual results are poor enough to resort to our contingency plan ("N + 1") which was formulated earlier in Step 12. The execution is easy, quick, and simple, because all that's needed is a comparison of actual results with the criteria we established in Step 15. Again, it is an impersonal, objective, quantitative decision.

Most important, this step prevents "gross errors." That is, by asking this question at this time, we preclude the possibility of a "surprise" financial disaster.

21. *Implement Minor Corrective Action*

If the answer to the question posed in Step 20 is NO, we proceed to take corrective managerial action. The action to be taken in this step is exceedingly difficult to predetermine. The action to be taken will depend on the frequency and severity that the array of actual results fall short of plan. There are too many possible scenarios to allow for earlier planning. It is simply not cost effective to explore them all, to anticipate the action to be taken in response to the myriad possible variations.

Management is, after all, an art. While professional, effective planning can contribute significantly to reducing many vagaries of management responses, management remains a nonmechanistic endeavor. Flexibility of choice of response to changing circumstances, which must be present to maximize effectiveness, *is* maintained by following this planning procedure.

The quality of the action taken by management is easily gauged by comparison of the results of action taken in this step with the organizational performance requirements quantified in Step 11.

Upon completion of the action initiated in this step, we return to Step 16 and continue implementation of Plan "N."

22. *Implement Plan "N + 1"*

If Step 20 tells us that the "N + 1" trigger should be pulled, we begin to implement Plan "N + 1," which was prepared during Steps 12, 13, and 14. Because the decision made in Step 20 was quantitative, impersonal, and objective, the implementation of "N + 1" can proceed quickly, unhampered by discussion and emotional exchanges. The speed with which "N + 1" can be implemented helps significantly to enhance likelihood of success.

23. *Formalize "Crash" Program*

24. *Quantify "Crash" Objectives*

25. *Quantify Organizational Performance Requirements*

26. *Quantify "Crash" Trigger*

Once "N + 1" has been launched, these four steps— identical in concept to Steps 12, 13, 14, and 15—quantitatively define the actions we will take and when we will take them if the actual results of "N + 1" action are sufficiently unfavorable to trigger the "crash" program.

27. *Measure Performance*

The output of this step is a periodic quantitative evaluation of actual performance. It is prepared in a manner identical to Step 17.

28. *Plan "N" Objectives Achieved?*

Performance recovery may be sufficiently strong to reach the levels objectified in the original Plan "N." If the answer is YES, we return to Step 8 to inquire whether the strategy goals were reached.

29. *Plan "N + 1" Objectives Achieved?*

If the answer to Step 28 is NO, then we want to ascertain whether the "N + 1" objectives were achieved. If they were, we proceed to Step 16 and continue implementation of Plan "N."

30. *Trigger "Crash" Program?*

We failed to reach both "N" and "N + 1" objectives. Consistent with the concept of Step 20, we want to know just how bad performance was. Comparison of actual results with the predetermined quantitative "crash" trigger (Step 26) will direct us either to take remedial action (the unfavorable deviation is *not* all that great) or to implement "crash" (we're really in trouble).

31. *Implement Minor Corrective Action*

Consistent with the concepts discussed earlier in Step 21, management takes the action that it feels will restore performance to "N + 1" objective levels. After the action has been implemented, we return to Step 22 and continue to operate the "N + 1" plan.

32. *Implement "Crash" Program*

If the results of Step 30 dictate the implementation of the "crash" program, we launch as soon as possible— the same day, even the same hour. We are able to take such immediate action because we formalized and documented that action earlier in Steps 23–26.

33. *Measure Performance*

The purpose and execution of this Step are identical to those discussed earlier in Steps 17 and 27.

34. *Plan "N" Objectives Achieved?*

As in Step 28 earlier, we compare performance first to the original plan objectives to ascertain whether substantial business health has been restored. If YES, we proceed to Step 8 to determine whether the original strategy goals have been achieved. If not, we proceed to test whether "N + 1" objectives have been reached.

35. *Plan "N + 1" Objectives Achieved?*

The test is performed in the same manner as earlier in Step 29. If the "N + 1" objectives *have* been reached, we proceed to Step 29, which, in turn, returns us to Step 16, where we resume implementation of Plan "N."

36. *"Crash" Program Objectives Achieved?*

If, in Step 35, we learned that the "N + 1" objectives were *not* achieved, our concern focuses on whether performance is at least at "crash" program objective levels. If

YES, we proceed to Step 22 and resume implementation of Plan "N + 1."

37. *Trigger Abort Program?*

If performance failed to meet "crash" program objectives in Step 36, we need to know whether performance was so poor as to pull the abort program trigger. Again, prompt, efficient decision-making is facilitated because the parameters were much earlier quantified in Step 2.

38. *Implement Minor Corrective Action*

The performance of this step identically parallels action discussed earlier for Steps 21 and 31.

Upon initiation of the management action, we return to Step 32 and continue implementation of the "crash" program.

39. *Implement Abort Program*

We have finally come to the step that we have taken thirty-eight earlier steps to avoid. We're at the point, now, where despite all of our "best laid schemes" our business has "gang a-gley."

The only solace that we can take rests in the knowledge that we have minimized our losses; we can *promptly* enact the abort program, because we have already prepared the detailed assignments to minimize adverse consequences.

PART IV

How to Plan an Ongoing Business

A

Preparing the Plan

The key to successful planning for an ongoing business is to decide what changes you make *today* so that results *tomorrow* will be different from (better than) those of *yesterday.*

This part is a natural follow-on to Part III. For this part it is assumed that the business has survived for most of the first year, that it looks healthy enough to keep going, and that we'd best start preparing for next year. The planning for next year must be done with the same care and thoroughness, of course, but the format and process are somewhat different. We *do* have some actual performance *data,* and we can fairly accurately forecast the remainder of the year. In a firm that has been in operation for several years, the planning for next year, if it's done at all, starts late in the third quarter, usually around August or September if the firm uses a calendar fiscal year.

Every autumn that time comes again when department heads, functional vice presidents, division presidents, and, yes, even group executives don their ballet slippers and tutus and begin the ritual of "Let's see how little *I* will be held accountable for!" It's called BUDGETING.

Studies have been made, of course, of the cost of purchasing versus purchase cost and the cost of cost accounting, and so on. While I have not seen studies on the cost of preparing a budget, I would guess that it is substantial, particularly if performed in the time-honored sequence of present/review, re-present/rereview, re-re-present/re-rereview—ad nauseam, all part of playing the game of "hide the fudge factor."

Preoccupation with the sales line (or any line other than pre-tax) leads to excessive, unnecessary, and unproductive bookkeeping exercises in preparing the basic fundamental documents: income statement, balance sheet, and cash (or funds) flow.

How does one cut through all the Mickey Mouse and get to the heart of the matter? How does one elevate the budgeting process from an accounting department add-on work task (ugh!) to an exercise of management challenge that results in a personal accountability to quantified "stretch" objectives upon which meaningful, impersonal incentive compensation can be based? Got your attention? Read on.

First of all the "boss" (the guy/gal in the "corner office": the Chairman, the C.E.O., or whatever title) sets the threshold of performance and the ground rules. Then subordinates develop their plans/strategies minimally to reach the threshold in conformance with the ground rules. Shown below is a list of some examples of them for you to use if you don't already have any of your own. Now, as you read through them, don't waste my time or yours by playing the "what if" game—you know, where you read the performance requirement and then lean back and say, "Hell, I can think of a case that can be constructed to support (or destroy) any position." You're not reading this book to try to win a debate with me. You're reading it to see if there is a way to avoid most of the nonsensical waste of time and money usually incurred in budget preparation. Well, there is a way. And if you don't have enough creativity, knowledgeability, and influence to effect favorable changes in your firm, stop reading right now. You will only be frustrated after all.

Some examples of sound, universally acceptable minimum performance thresholds are listed below in no particular order of priority:

- Selling price increases will at least keep pace with inflation.
- Selling price action will be based on "what the market will bear," not as markup from cost.
- Profitability will improve over prior period, whether measured as Return on Sales or, preferably, as Return on Investment.
- Cost reduction programs will at least offset effects of inflation and/or contractual obligations.

Notice that they all have one thing in common: They all are addressed solely to pre-tax effects. Not market share, not sales, not anything else. Bankers and financial analysists have deep, abiding interest *only* in profit-per-share; they have *no* interest in market-share-per-share or anything-else-per-share. Shareholders should also be similarly interested; too often they are not, but that's another book.

Because the cardinal interest and focus is at the pre-tax line, it logically follows that the budget process should begin with an "Analysis of Changes in Operating Pre-Tax." Until that analysis and the consequent projection is accepted, it is pointless and a waste of precious time and money to prepare any of the detailed financials. It should be the first form used in budget preparation.

It is obviously impossible to present a meaningful planning procedure, for every type of firm in every type of business, within the covers of a single book. I chose the context of a manufacturing firm largely because my experience in management has dealt exclusively with this type of business. So, incorporating the Principles in Part I, let's proceed to examine in detail how to develop an effective year-to-year profit plan.

A sample of a particularly useful form for this purpose is shown in Figure 2. It is uniquely relevant to firms that manufacture and sell products, but similar ones can be (and have been) developed for service firms. Lines 1 through 23 display a typical or traditional income statement format. Columns A and W are used to record the prior year actual/forecast and budget year projection, respectively. Columns B through V are used to show the respective line-item pre-tax changes that lead from current year to budget year. A support form should be used to highlight further the changes in operating pre-tax in the "below the line" expense categories, such as Operations Management, Engineering Sales (or Distribution), and General/Administrative. In some firms, Operations Management may be included in the Burden pool. Nonetheless, it is useful for profit-planning purposes to highlight this often significant expense to avoid losing actual expense control while exploring the "absorption effect" measurement. Also, it is useful for profit-planning purposes to highlight (also for control purposes) the total expenses, however reclassified.

First of all, be mindful that even with the most thorough and complete utilization, most of the intersectional cells will be blanks. In other words don't allow your subordinates to be overawed by the mere appearance of the form (of course, *you* won't be). This is *not* a "government" form, where it is required that all of the blanks be filled in.

Second, note that it is *not* an accounting form. It is aimed at communication at the management level. It provides for a blend of traditional accounting system data and nonaccounting system data/treatment, such as population levels and the ground rule that parentheses *always* means *unfavorable* (all together now—hooray!—from those of us who always have trouble keeping it straight!).

Third, it is *not* a "magic" form. It is only *a* version of what you should refine or tailor to suit the needs of your particular firm. Nor will filling it out and filing it away result in objective achievement. It is, after all, only a tool. And how you, as the craftsman, *use* that tool will really determine what the end results will be.

The professional, effective planner will use it, certainly,

			SALES				LABOR				MATERIAL
							COST INCREASE		COST REDUCTION		PRICE
	BASE YEAR	VOLUME	MIX	PRICE	POPULATION	WAGES	POPULATION	WAGES	MIX	INCREASE	COST REDUCTION
	A	B	C	D	E	F	G	H	I	J	K
1. Gross Sales											
2. Returns and Allowances											
3. Net Sales											
4. Commissions											
5. NAC Sales											
6. Standard Cost of Sales											
7. Standard Margin											
8. Labor Variance											
9. Material Variance											
10. Burden Variance											
11. Gross Margin											
12. Obsolescence											
13. Warranty											
14. Total Cost of Sales											
15. Net Return on Sales											
16. Operations Management											
17. Engineering: In-house											
18. Engineering: Contract											
19. Total Engineering											
20. Selling Expense											
21. Administrative Expense											
22. Total "Below the Line"											
23. Operating Pre-tax											

Figure 2. Analysis of Changes in Operating Pre-Tax

110

	BURDEN							BELOW THE LINE EXPENSES				
COST INCREASES			COST REDUCTION									
POPULATION	WAGES	OTHER EXPENSES	POPULATION	WAGES	OTHER EXPENSES	OPERATIONS MANAGEMENT	ENGINEERING	SELLING	ADMINISTRATIVE	DIFFERENCE	PLAN YEAR	
L	M	N	O	P	Q	R	S	T	U	V	W	

as a means of establishing (or embellishing) his organizational power. It provides the essentials for successful establishment (or reinforcement) of superior–subordinate relationships.

I prefer to tie in the quantitative intersectional cell data, first to an Incentive Compensation Plan (objective not subjective, measurable, and all that good stuff) and second to the monthly management report. Okay, it's time to start walking through the form to make sure that we really understand it. Let's begin with the column headings.

The Columns

1. *Effect of Sales on Pre-Tax*

Columns B, C, and D present, respectively, the budgeted *changes* (both favorable and unfavorable) from prior year, in volume, mix, and price. Thus, direct measurable clarity is focused on what otherwise is at best a "fuzzy" number. Volume and mix projections can be interrogated back into the supporting plans for order intake, which, in turn, can be further traced into the supporting sales promotion and new product plans to ensure harmoney and consistency in both timing and dollars.

Targeting a specific price effect provides managerial audit of the pricing program to ensure timing and adequacy of amount of increase, to ensure capture so that, in turn, the planned pre-tax contribution is achieved.

2. *Effect of Manufacturing Cost on Pre-Tax*

Columns E through Q provide for display of specifics relative to budgeted behavior of the three prime cost elements, Labor, Material, and Burden. Labor covers Columns E, F, G, and H. The pattern of analysis for both Labor and Burden, as we shall see later, is the same, namely, first the identification of elements that *increase* cost, then identification of cost reduction goals to *offset* the cost increases. First the "bad news," then the "good news." For Labor analysis, both population and wages are shown. Thus inferences can be quantified relative to average wages paid and effect on efficiency (by cross-reference to Line 8, Labor Variance); insight is gained into the burden absorption base (cross-referencing population with Line 10, Burden Variance) and labor efficiency levels identified earlier; and so on. Similarly, the aggressiveness of planned cost reduction is more visible through study of Columns G and H, both in absolute terms and in comparative or relative terms by cross-reference to population per cent changes, which are affected by cost reduction, and so on.

The key determinants of Material Cost are Mix (Column I) and Price (Columns J and K). In each of these instances, quantified projections are required to show both the unfavorable *and* the favorable budgeted performances.

Burden Cost (Columns L through Q) is analyzed again from both the Increases and the Cost Reduction viewpoints, again relating population levels to expense levels. Columns N and Q, Other Expenses are *not* meant to mean "miscellaneous"; they include all expenses not directly related to population. The numbers can be quite large.

3. *Effect of "Below the Line" Expenses on Pre-Tax*

Columns R through U present both the favorable and the unfavorable effects on planned performance. In each case, population levels must be related to dollar expense levels for managerial "reasonability testing."

Column V is used to display the summed changes recorded in Columns B through U. Column W is derived by combining Columns A and V.

The Lines

Now let's proceed *down* the Income Statement, *line by line*. Lines 1 through 5 deal exclusively with Sales. Returns and Allowances, and Commissions are deducted from Gross Sales to arrive at Net After Commission (NAC) Sales. They interface with Columns B, C, and D.

Lines 6 through 10 evaluate Cost of Goods Sold so that, by subtraction, the Gross Margin, Line 11, is generated. Figure 2 is designed to accommodate a standard cost system. If you use another costing method, merely substitute the appropriate lines. Inferences drawn from intersectional entries on the Variance lines (8, 9, and 10) are particularly useful. Insight into the planned changes, for example, in labor efficiency can be gained by study of the entries in the Labor Variance–Population (or Line 8–Column G) intersection.

Given steady or rising volume (Column B), decreases in population should improve Labor Variance, or at least reduce the adverse effect of increased wages (Column F).

Line 11, Gross Margin, is sometimes called Factory Profit. To obtain Total Cost of Sales (or Cost of Goods Sold), provision for Obsolescence (Line 12) and Warranty (line 13) costs are subtracted from Gross Margin (Line 11).

The Net Return on Sales (Line 15) shows the gross profit available to cover operating expenses and operating pre-tax.

Lines 16 through 21 show planned behavior of the Below the Line expenses. Line 16, Operations Management, assumes that production control/scheduling, purchasing, industrial or manufacturing engineering, and so on are treated as period or line item expenses. This simply means that they are not included in the burden pool and incorporated into inventory via burden absorption. This is probably the most conservative treatment. It keeps these costs out of the balance sheet and retains them in the income statement. It tends to reduce reported operating pre-tax, particularly if volume is sufficiently high to permit overabsorption.

Lines 17 and 18 provide means to analyze Engineering expense from both the In-House and Contract viewpoints. Selling Expense (Line 20) includes marketing, advertising, promotion, shows, conventions, and so on, as well as direct selling expenses. More discussion will follow a little later on how to tailor Figure 2 to your particular firm.

Administrative Expense (Line 21) includes the usual assortment of accounting, finance, administrative, accrual, interest, and other expenses. Line 22 (Total "Below the Line") is the sum of lines 16 through 21 and is subtracted from Line 15 (Net Return on Sales) to arrive, finally, at Operating Pre-Tax, Line 23.

So much for the "nuts and bolts" about Figure 2. Now that the two of you have been properly introduced, let us talk for a while about some relationships and concepts that will enable you to *use* Figure 2 more effectively.

B

Evaluating the Plan

First of all, evaluate the "health" of your planned business. The best way to diagnose the vitality of your plan for the upcoming year is to quantify comparative productivity measures. While there are many such measures, the most important ones, with respect to Figure 2, are:

1. Sales $ per employee
2. Pre-tax $ per employee
3. Compensation $ as percent of sales $
4. Compensation $ per employee

The value of these ratios should be calculated for all prior years, the year ending, and the plan year. In this manner trend behavior is easily discerned. A brief discussion of each ratio will be helpful. Recall that we are planning for a manufacturing firm.

1. Sales $ per Employee

Use *net* sales dollars (Line 3 on Figure 2). It is only from net revenue that profits can be generated. Naturally, the higher the value the better. However, if the ratio value drops below $25,000, there are serious questions to be asked. A "good" performance would be in the range of $30,000–$35,000.

The important point is that it increases each successive year or that there are compelling reasons to explain the failure satisfactorily.

2. Pre-Tax $ per Employee

Again, the higher the better. Again, this ratio should improve each successive year. The minimum acceptable level should be $5,000 or so. A "good" ratio value is in the range of $7,500–$12,000.

3. Compensation $ as Percent of Sales $

When calculating this ratio, include *all* compensation. That is, include all elements and costs of compensation; wages, salaries, fringes, vacation, and so on. Clearly the lower the ratio the better. And again, the trend should reveal a decreasing value each successive year. To reveal such a trend, the increase in sales dollars (resulting from a combination of higher volume and higher prices as shown in Columns B and D in Figure 2) must be greater, proportionately, than the increase in compensation dollars. Or, because of labor-saving capital investment or other reduction in population (Columns G and O in Figure 2), the number of compensation dollars decreases.

A "good" performance is in the 30–33 percent range.

4. Compensation $ per Employee

In this case, lower is *not* necessarily better! The nature of the products the firm makes and sells may require compensation levels somewhat higher than other firms with similar sales levels.

The "normal" trend is an increase in each successive year. The comparison should be made to the rate of inflation. If the Compensation $ per Employee rises faster than inflation or is planned to rise faster than inflation, a number of serious questions must be raised.

I shall next introduce you to a number of "sanity checks." The purpose of a "sanity check" is to force consideration of the compatibility (or lack thereof) between the plan and basic relationships that exist in manufacturing business. Before even submitting the plan, be sure that the implementation consequences and inferences are in harmony with these "sanity checks"; if not, have some really good answers handy!

Sanity Check No. 1:   The Profitable Use of Stocking Distributors Is Inversely Proportional to the Engineering Content in the Product

Another way to say this is: The greater the engineering content in the product, the less profitable it will be to try to route it to market through stocking distributors. The relationship is illustrated in Graph A. Note that what's important is the engineering content in *each* product. In other words, while millions may have been expended in research and development, if the result is a "standard" product, *each* of which bears little technical cost, then use of stocking distributors is appropriate.

The greater the engineering content in each product sold, the greater the need for direct sales efforts.

A final noteworthy inference is that, absent other considerations, the greater the number of units of products sold annually, the greater the profitability potential by use of stocking distributors. Thus, even if vast sums are initially spent for technical development, the large number of unit sales means that the engineering content in each unit is relatively small; there are more units over which to spread the investment.

Graph A

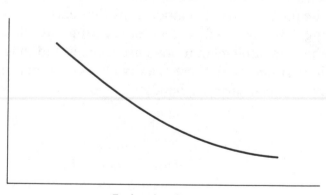

Engineering Content

Don't try to sell spaceships through stocking distributors! Don't try to sell nuts and bolts through direct salesmen!

Sanity Check No. 2: Product Cost Reduction Potential Is Inversely Related to Product Engineering Content

In Figure 2, Columns G, H, K, O, P, and Q pinpoint the planned pre-tax improvements based on Cost Reduction. This sanity check points directly at Labor Costs (Columns G and H) and Material Costs (Column K).

The relationship that this sanity check identifies is illustrated in Graph B. Usually product performance requirements—reliability, product life, quality, and so on—demand more engineering content as they are made more rigorous. In other words, products costs are less important than product performance. Further, plans to reduce significantly the costs of a product with a large engineering content are precarious. They must rely on achieving sig-

Graph B

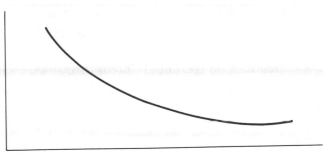

Product Cost Reduction Potential

nificant advances in state of the art. The probability of such achievement within the forced time frame of a plan period is certainly not high. Therefore, to the extent that the planned pre-tax is based on such cost improvements, the entire planned pre-tax is jeopardized and highly suspect.

Sanity Check No. 3: *Product Cost Reduction Potential Is Directly Proportional to Quantity of Product Sold*

The more you produce and sell of the same (or very similar) items, the more realistic it is to depend on (demand, even) pre-tax improvement by product cost reduction. If the volume is large enough, reductions of fractions of a penny add up to big numbers.

Aside from the sheer volume effect, the sureness of capture of cost reduction is enhanced by the operation of two underlying principles. First, the increment of cost reduction per unit can be very small, hence should be relatively easy to accomplish. It should be easy to identify, monitor, and implement. Only minor investments in tools, jigs, dies, fixtures, and workstation modification are required and usually will yield appealing returns. The second principle is that achievement of cost reduction is *not* dependent on technical "breakthroughs." The owners of the business need not agonize over the descent of the inspirational muses.

The volume effect, of course, should yield favorable purchase terms. Given sufficient volume, relatively modest investments in the cost of purchasing usually generate significant improvements in unit purchase cost.

All of this is *not* to say that technical investments should *not* be made. It may very well be the case that significant engineering investments should be made—to effect strategic and profound cost reduction by material substitution, for instance. But don't plan on realizing those big pre-tax bucks unless you're on the verge of making the change.

One final point to consider is that the greater the unit volume, the greater the potential for substitution of labor by capital equipment. However, if labor cost is less than, say 10 percent of total unit cost, don't rank capital projects high on the priority list.

Sanity Check No. 4: Profitable Investment in Finished Goods Inventory Is Inversely Related to Product Engineering Content

The inventory profile of a manufacturing firm warrants considerable attention. The traditional definition of "inventory profile" is the amount of investment, respectively, in raw materials, work in process, and finished goods.

The relationship of engineering content to the relative proportion of finished goods inventory can best be illustrated as in Graph C. The greater the engineering content in the product, the less investment in finished goods inventory you should make. As a corollary, the greater the engineering content in the product, the larger, relatively, should be the investment in raw material.

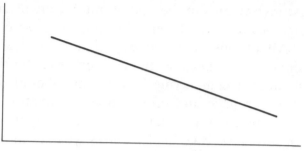

Graph C

A large engineering content in a product presupposes a great deal of customization of the delivered product. Therefore, prudence dictates that investment in finished goods be kept to a minimum so as (1) to better serve the market for finished goods and (2) to avoid exposure to technological obsolescence.

Thus, the critical balance sheet inference from Figure 2 is that if the nature of the product(s) involved in your business requires considerable engineering content, next year's plan should reveal a profile of inventory that shows a relatively high profile of raw material, a (much) lower work in process, and (practically) zero finished goods. The converse is always equally true.

Sanity Check No. 5: The Degree of Management Effectiveness Is Inversely Proportional to Span of Control

The larger the number of people supervised, the less effectively will they be managed. The basic veracity of this rule is borne out in real-life situations where managers

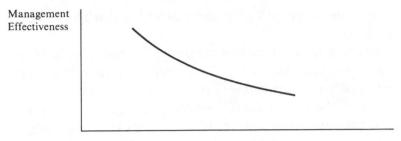

Span of Control

Graph D

find that monitoring and follow-up become increasingly difficult as the number of immediate subordinates increases. The relationship is illustrated in Graph D.

Management is, after all, the art of getting work done through the efforts of others. The more "others" there are to keep track of, to motivate, to train and to develop, to discipline, and so on, the greater the effort needed to extract the "best" that *each* of the subordinates is able to perform.

Look, then, to the supporting documents of Figure 2. Insist that organization charts accompany the Figure 2 submittal. Scrutinize those charts with great care and in close detail. Examine the changes (if any) in span of control. If it is enlarged, insist on explanation of why management effectiveness will not be sufficiently diluted thereby to jeopardize success of the plan.

Sanity Check 6: Retraining Difficulty of Personnel Is Directly Proportional to Tenure

Everybody resists change. How often have you heard that old saw? Too often? Well, maybe it's not so! Not everybody resists change to the same extent and with the same intensity!

Retraining is ultimately necessary if your firm is growing. The basic meaning of "growth" is new products, new markets, acquisitions, divestitures, or combinations of all of them. "Growth" presupposes going where the firm has never been before. If a firm does indeed go where it has not yet been, change is not only inevitable, it is imminent.

Of importance to us is the reality that the newer members in the organization are less concerned about change than those who have lengthy tenure. Why is that so? The basic principle is: The less you have at stake or at risk, the less you really care about any changes that may eventuate.

The long-tenured employee, unfortunately, *feels* that he has a great deal "invested." The way the firm works is familiar to him. Change represents a disturbance to "the way things are done around here." The longer the tenure of the employee, the more threatened he feels about a potential change. Will his skills be needed? Will his "status" be diminished? Where will he end up *after* the change occurs? The important point to consider is *not* the answers to those questions! The important point is that *questions* are raised. The more questions raised, the greater the degree of uncertainty that exists. And loss of "certainty" or at least predictability is the birth of anxiety.

There is no argument that the greater the anxiety, the greater the stress. And the greater the stress, the greater the opposition. So, to the extent that next year's plan represents change, inquire as to the tenure of the affected individuals to ascertain the scope and intensity of resistance.

Sanity Check No. 7: A Little Personnel Turnover Helps Profitability, a Lot Hurts

Take a look at Graph E right away, because this sanity check is a little tricky. An organization is akin to a tree. If no pruning is done at all, the tree will most probably be stunted and diseased, and will prematurely lose its vigor and die. If pruned too deeply and too often, it will never even get started!

It has often been said that there are old pilots and there are bold pilots, but there are *no* old *and* bold pilots! The very same is true of organizations! There are old (and usually unprofitable) organizations. There are bold (and usually profitable) organizations. But there are absolutely *no* old *and* bold organizations.

Financial performance results only from the action of people—of the organization. Excellent performance can

Graph E

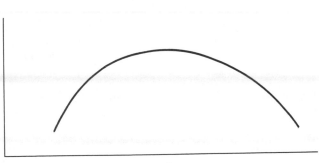

Personnel Turnover

only be attained by excellent people, an excellent organization. Achieving new, higher levels of profitability can be done only by a *bold* organization!

It has been said that "there *will* come a time when no single incumbent will occupy his present position." This is *not* a fatuous observation. It is recognition of the inevitability of turnover. The task of management is *not* to try to forestall the inevitable. Rather, the prime task of management is to *control* the timing, rate, and scope of turnover!

Thus, if one of the basic premises of next year's performance is tied too tightly to no or extremely low personnel turnover, look hard at the probability of success. Remember, tenure does *not* equal experience!

On the other hand, too much turnover can indeed cripple the performance of an organization. While organizational pruning, up to a point, can actually contribute to plan success, too much turnover can, in fact, jeopardize success. Too many people on the "learning curve" at one time will brake the firm's progress.

The bottom line? You're *not* maximizing organizational competence if turnover equals zero!

Sanity Check No. 8:   Too Much Bad Debt Expense Hurts Profitability—but So Does Too Little

The management that prides itself on having "zero" bad debt expense is *not* optimizing profitability! It's as simple as that. Owners are being gypped even if management is planning to incur zero bad debt expense. Why is this so?

When credit extension requirements become *so* restrictive as to preclude exposure to bad debts, it is axiomatic that sales are far from maximized. Socrates speaks to managers from more than two thousand years ago when he admonishes, "Moderation in all things." A little bad debt expense is healthy. It means that management is exploiting sales opportunities. The debt expense relationship to profitability of the firm can be shown as in Graph F.

Thus, when bad debt expense is held to extremely low levels, it unduly restricts billings, which lowers the firm's profitability. And when bad debt expense becomes too large, not only is short-term profitability damaged, but the very existence of the firm is in jeopardy. When, to obtain sales, too frequent extension of credit to questionable credit customers occurs, several inferences regarding the viability of the firm can be made.

First and foremost, the extent to which the firm is outperformed by its competitors must be examined in deep detail. Look first to the degree to which your firm's products compete successfully with those of the competi-

Graph F

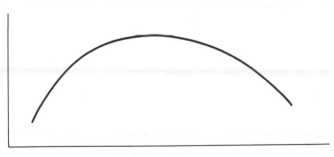

Profitability of the Firm

Bad Debt Expense

tion. Only rarely does bad debt expense reach intolerable levels because of poor credit management performance or a breakdown in credit approval procedures. It is almost always the case that competition is outproductizing your firm. Your management thus has no more desirable alternative than to try for sales growth by accepting orders from more and more unreliably paying customers.

If bad debt expense is too low, loosen the credit controls a little. If bad debt expense is too large, hurry to develop new and better-performing products!

PART V

How to Plan a New Product

For purposes of this part, it is assumed that all the traditional marketing and sales analyses have already been performed. That is, it is assumed that the market needs have been identified, that product specifications have been prepared to at least a semidetailed level, that pricing guidelines have been set, that distribution channels and product characteristics are not in disharmony, and so on. A great deal of homework must already have been performed. It is not necessary that all or even most of the homework have been formalized and documented. What *is* important is that the planner be as certain as possible that he has properly and thoroughly defined a viable solution to a real, live market need.

Of the three operational planning areas presented in this book, planning a new product is probably the most difficult. That does not mean intellectually difficult, although new product planning certainly tests the limits of the planner's anticipatorial skills. The planner must quantitatively describe *two* scenarios simultaneously. The essence of new product planning consists of evaluating the financial results generated by two distinct courses of action. The first course of action is to *not* introduce the new product. The second course is to introduce it. The new product plan, then, takes the form of a "Without the New Product," "With the New Product," "Due to the New Product" analysis.

There are only two sets or packages of planning documents that you really need. First is the Financial Plan. Essentially, this comprises a comparative Income Statement and a comparative Investment Analysis. The purpose is to evaluate results with the new product, results without it, and the incremental results of the introduction of it.

The second set or package is the Technical Plan. The need for this set is directly proportional to extent to which engineering development is required to bring the new product to market. In other words, the greater the need for involvement of technical/engineering personnel and performance to develop the new product, the more detail and care is required to document the Technical Plan effectively.

A

The Financial Plan

The essential document of the Financial Plan is the Comparative Income Statement. It consists of three sections, all in the traditional income statement currently used in your firm. There is no need to develop a unique form. Use of the familiar format enhances understanding.

All three should be expressed in the same interval of projection. That is, whether the selected plan period is two, three, or five years, all three income statements should reflect the same period. Except in very unusual situations, any period shorter than three years is too short; any period longer than five years is too long. For manufacturing firms, a period of five years seems to be most useful.

Figure 3 presents an example of a form that is particularly useful for this exercise. Note its universality. That is, Figure 3 can be used successfully to analyze not only new product projects, but capital expenditure projects, asset sales, and virtually any major project that may affect

PROJECT TITLE _____ PROJECT NO. _____ DATE _____

134

LIFE OF PROJECT	BEFORE PROJECT IS OPERATIONAL		AFTER PROJECT IS OPERATIONAL							
	1st YEAR	2nd YEAR	1st YEAR 19 __	2nd YEAR 19 __	3rd YEAR 19 __	4th YEAR 19 __	5th YEAR 19 __	6th YEAR To Complete 19 __	TOTAL PROJECT	AVERAGE YEAR
WITH THE PROJECT										
1 Sales										
2 Material Costs										
3 Depreciation & Amortization										
4 Other Operating Costs										
5 Marketing & A&G Expenses										
6 Net Profit after Taxes										
7 Net Current Assets										
8 Net Cash Surplus (Requirements)										
9 Return on Assets %										
10 Return on Sales %										
WITHOUT THE PROJECT										
1 Sales										
2 Material Costs										
3 Depreciation & Amortization										
4 Other Operating Costs										
5 Marketing & A&G Expenses										
6 Net Profit after Taxes										
7 Net Current Assets										
8 Net Cash Surplus (Requirements)										
9 Return on Assets %										
10 Return on Sales %										

	DUE TO THE PROJECT														
1	Sales														
2	Material Costs														
3	Depreciation & Amortization														
4	Other Operating Costs														
5	Marketing & A&G Expenses														
6	Gross Profit Before Taxes														
7	Capital Expenditures-Net														
8	Net Current Assets														
9	Related Project Expenses														
10	TOTAL PROJECT INVESTMENT														
11	Net Cash Surplus (Requirements)														
12	Cumulative Cash Surplus (Reqmts.)														
13	Assets Transferred to Project														
14	Return on Assets %														
15	Return on Sales %														
16	Payback Period—Years														
17	Return on Investment %														

Figure 3. Comparative Income Statement Form

the Income Statement, Balance Sheet, or Cash Flow of the firm.

The second income statement can be lifted, virtually intact, from your firm's Five-year Business Plan if you're fortunate enough to have one. This projected statement displays the anticipated results of operations without the proposed new product.

Considerable market analysis and study are required to prepare five-year projections with the new product. The first task, of course, is to measure market assessment of the acceptance of the new product. While there is no single "magic" outline or format that can be universally applied, the Marketing Plan Checklist provides a uniquely effective first step. All the key information you will need is yours when you finish playing "twenty questions." The checklist has been referred to as "What I Always Wanted to Know About My Markets, But Never Knew What to Ask." Finding and documenting the answers is essentially nothing more than labor. You will discover that most of the answers are readily available in one form or another. The difficult task is *not* getting the answers—it's knowing the questions that *must* be asked!

There are only two possible sources of sales of new products. Either the new product will be sold to the current served market, or it will be sold to a new market segment. If your new product plan is the former, you need to do hardly any review at all of Questions 1, 2, and 3. As a matter of fact, the answers to most of the questions will be pretty much the same. However, of great importance *and* key to your *With–Without–Due to* analysis are the answers to the numerous subquestions of Question 8, "What Will This Do to Our Other Products?"

Pivotal to the analysis is the evaluation of the extent of product substitutability. But above all, the ultimate justification of the introduction of a new product is to enhance the enduring value of the owner's investment!

If your new product plan is based on penetration of a new market segment, however, start with Question 1 and don't omit any questions at all.

MARKETING PLAN CHECKLIST

1. *What Do We Have to Sell? For How Long?*
   name
   function
   use
   expected life cycle
   special features
   etc.
2. *To Whom Will We Sell It?*
   composition
   size
   geographic location
   characteristics
   requirements
   names of specific people, if possible
3. *What Is Our Competition?*
   names
   feature and use comparison
   price comparison
   delivery comparison
4. *What Are We Trying to Accomplish?*
   statement of objectives
   product sales in units, dollars, and market share by varying
     time period

5. *What Techniques Will We Use?*
    costs (by increments)
    pricing philosophy
    distribution plan by geographical area
    marketing theme and basic product appeal to customer
    delivery schedules
    payment terms
    guarantees and warranty
    tie-in sales
6. *How Will We Introduce the Product?*
    launch program
        in-house sales force
        distributors
        product announcement
    sales call plan
7. *How Do We Motivate the Sales Force?*
    incentive programs
        a. regional and individual quotas
        b. commissions
        c. contests
        d. special promotions, etc.
    reporting
8. *What Will This Do to Our Other Products?*
    volumes
    units
    redesign of other products in line to match new one
    inventory reduction of old stock
9. *Why, What, When and How Are We Going to Advertise?*
    objectives
    budget
    major and minor themes
    ad schedules
    strategy and schedule for relating ad program to field sales
        effort
10. *Can We "Rifle" as Well as "Shotgun" the Market?*
    objectives
    budget

mailing list
strategy and schedule for relating direct mail program to field
sales effort

11. *How to Play "Host" with Maximum Return? (How Much*
"E" of "T and E"?)
objectives
budget
schedule of events and dates
themes
invitation lists
strategy and schedules for utilizing participation for maximum
field sales effort
follow-up plans

12. *How Can We Get Additional Exposure?*
objectives
budget
themes
techniques
outside agency
press releases
technical papers
etc.

13. *How Do We Train Our Own People to Sell the Products?*
objectives
budget
techniques
schedule
props and publications needed; schedule for obtaining

14. *How Do We Teach the Customer the Use and Benefits of*
the Product?
objectives
budget
techniques
schedule
props and publications needed; schedule of obtaining

15. *How Are We Going to Organize to Keep the Product Operating in Warranty?*
    policy
    strategy for use as sales tool
    anticipated cost

16. *What Are We Going to Do and How After Warranty Expires?*
    policy
    strategy for use as sales tool
    budgeted cost or sales and profit

17. *How Do We Use Spare Parts to Build Sales and Profits?*
    distribution policy
    pricing policy
    strategy
    budgeted sales and profit

18. *How Will We Inform Prospects?*
    catalogs, spec sheets, tech. manuals, other publications, etc.
    quantity
    distribution
    schedule

19. *How Do We Support Sales Effort with Product?*
    policy
    levels
    strategy

20. *What "Props" Will the Sales Force Need—and When?*
    models or samples
    films and film-showing equipment
    drawing and blueprints
    pictures
    advertising portfolio
    visual sales presentation
    other new equipment
    testimonial letters
    documented profit and/or savings presentation
    etc.

To recall, the second income statement was based on *no* new product, essentially projection of an "as is" condition. We're ready now to prepare the first income statement. This income statement focuses exclusively on new product sales. Typically, new product sales are projected with the growth curve shown in Graph G.

Growth rate is usually modest in the first two and sometimes three years. However, growth rises almost geometrically after the new product is firmly entrenched. Obviously, there can be many variations on the shape of this curve. Among the major factors are (1) the magnitude of the need (or problem) of the served market and (2) the scope and effectiveness of the introduction of the new product to the market. In general, however, if the growth curve is significantly more accelerated than the "traditional" curve, it means that numerous tough questions must be asked to assure plan realism.

The third income statement, finally, represents the "dif-

Graph G

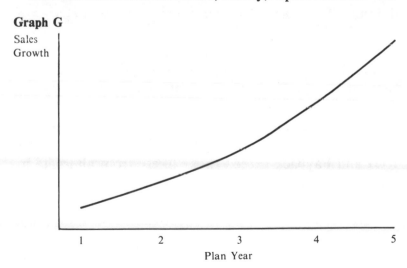

ference" between the first two. Actually, the third income statement is a combination of the first two. It quantifies the answers to Question 8. It is essential that operating pre-tax income increase over the planning period. Further, and to be discussed in more detail later, operating pre-tax must increase at an incrementally greater rate than that offered by alternate investment. Operating pre-tax can improve over the "as is" projection in only four ways. The first, of course, is an increase of unit volume. The second is to avoid or mitigate decreasing unit volume. Third, the new product can provide savings either in manufacturing costs or in distribution costs, perhaps both. Fourth, even with no changes in unit volume or costs, the new product can command a higher price, usually because of an enhanced array of product performance features. The "ideal" new product, then, will command a higher price, cost less, *and* increase unit volume.

Having isolated the Income Statement effects of introduction of the new product, then, we are prepared to complete the Financial Plan. The next steps are similarly to prepare a "Due To" Balance Sheet and a "Due To" Cash Flow. There is nothing unique required in the analysis. Again, use of the existing statement format is appropriate—probably even mandatory.

Finally, the "Due To" Return on Investment and the "Due To" Payback can be prepared. To the extent that ROI and Payback exceed those likely from alternate investment plans, the likelihood of approval rises. Also, the less the absolute amounts required for investments, the greater the likelihood of approval.

B

The Technical Plan

In the context of a manufacturing firm, the introduction of a new product presupposes the technical development of the new product. The principal aim of this section is *not* to explore aspects of the technical work that are or might be required. Rather, our aim is to discuss the principal tasks dealing with the management and planning of the development effort.

Product development really begins with identification of product *performance* specifications, not *technical* specifications. It matters little whether the performance requirements emanate from the sales department, the engineering department, the finance department, or even the board chairman's office. The most useful way to define performance specifications is to display them as solutions to current problems. If the present product doesn't operate, say, fast enough, a performance specification or requirement could be expressed as a higher speed.

Another way to make performance specification lists more useful is to express them as ranges, or to boundarize them either by "threshold" minimums or "ceiling" maximums. Technical development efforts will be proportionally more productive as performance specifications are quantitatively expressed. The least useful guideline or directive is: Make the product "more reliable."

The most effective utilization of technical resources is based on project approval and control. Careful definition of the planned milestones and costs, incorporated in a project reporting system, virtually precludes unfavorable major surprises. Making specific individual assignments leads to meaningful status/prognosis reporting by key individuals. On the premise that these fundamental management controls are in place, Figure 4 depicts a "typical" flow chart upon which to base a Technical Plan.

Note the recurring involvement of engineering and other technical personnel until the First Production Run has been successfully completed. Note also that only the Prime Responsibility of individuals has been identified. It shows an iterative process, of course. Again, Figure 4 probably is not the complete answer for you to complete your particular plan. But one thing is sure: It will give you a sound head start.

A few final comments about engineering/technical personnel resources. There are only three sources of the people/services you will need to introduce your new product successfully. The first source is in-house. That is, they are employees of the firm. Favoring this approach is the premise of continuity of knowledge as the product moves from the laboratory through the plant to the final user. All things considered, this source usually is the least ex-

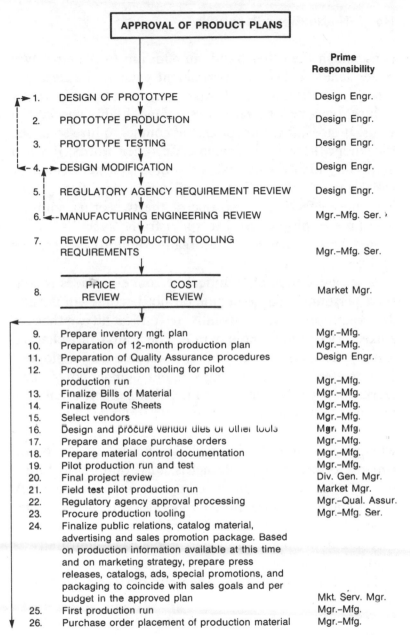

			Prime Responsibility
1.	DESIGN OF PROTOTYPE		Design Engr.
2.	PROTOTYPE PRODUCTION		Design Engr.
3.	PROTOTYPE TESTING		Design Engr.
4.	DESIGN MODIFICATION		Design Engr.
5.	REGULATORY AGENCY REQUIREMENT REVIEW		Design Engr.
6.	MANUFACTURING ENGINEERING REVIEW		Mgr.–Mfg. Ser.
7.	REVIEW OF PRODUCTION TOOLING REQUIREMENTS		Mgr.–Mfg. Ser.
8.	PRICE REVIEW	COST REVIEW	Market Mgr.
9.	Prepare inventory mgt. plan		Mgr.–Mfg.
10.	Preparation of 12-month production plan		Mgr.–Mfg.
11.	Preparation of Quality Assurance procedures		Design Engr.
12.	Procure production tooling for pilot production run		Mgr.–Mfg.
13.	Finalize Bills of Material		Mgr.–Mfg.
14.	Finalize Route Sheets		Mgr.–Mfg.
15.	Select vendors		Mgr.–Mfg.
16.	Design and procure vendor dies or other tools		Mgr. Mfg.
17.	Prepare and place purchase orders		Mgr.–Mfg.
18.	Prepare material control documentation		Mgr.–Mfg.
19.	Pilot production run and test		Mgr.–Mfg.
20.	Final project review		Div. Gen. Mgr.
21.	Field test pilot production run		Market Mgr.
22.	Regulatory agency approval processing		Mgr.–Qual. Assur.
23.	Procure production tooling		Mgr.–Mfg. Ser.
24.	Finalize public relations, catalog material, advertising and sales promotion package. Based on production information available at this time and on marketing strategy, prepare press releases, catalogs, ads, special promotions, and packaging to coincide with sales goals and per budget in the approved plan		Mkt. Serv. Mgr.
25.	First production run		Mgr.–Mfg.
26.	Purchase order placement of production material		Mgr.–Mfg.

Figure 4. New Product Introduction Flow Chart

145

pensive. On the other hand, an addition to the employee roster tends to become permanent even if the need for that person diminishes. Also, it may be extremely costly to hire someone who possesses unique, highly specialized skills. Besides, it is imprudent, of course, to hire someone for whom the need is episodic. In other words, if when a specific, identifiable task or problem is performed or solved, the need for that specialization disappears, then it is more effective to tap one of the two other sources. Full-time employees tend to suffer from "NIH"—not invented here. They may not really want to change the product.

A second source of technical personnel services is contract personnel. These people do not become employees. They perform services, usually at your facility, either for a fixed price or at an hourly rate. The hourly rate charged usually far exceeds the hourly rate paid to employees. The greater the engineering content demanded of their work, the less prudent it is to use them. Their seemingly higher rate of pay will antagonize permanent employees and their (hoped-for) early rather than late departure will cause disruption of knowledge continuity. An excellent use of contract personnel is, for example, to hire a few contract draftsmen to complete a measured stack of drawings under the direct supervision of the manager of drafting. Another example is resolution of an isolated, specialized problem for which knowledge continuity is relatively unimportant.

The third source is the design and development house. a corporation whose business it is to transform a set of performance specifications into, usually, a preproduction prototype. Such outfits may command expertise in electronics hardware and software and mechanical design and development. Patents and other proprietary information developed during the project become the property of the firm that engages them. They are a particularly effective source (1) when the product you seek is truly an advancement of the state of the art and/or a drastic change from current technology, such as when the new product is a transformation of a mechanical product to an electronic product, or (2) when design and development require specialized, expensive equipment.

In summary, the selection of the source of technical services is best governed by the nature of the project. The larger the number of project dollars involved and/or the greater the impact on sales of existing products, the more prudent it is likely to be to use a blend of all three—at different levels of involvement at different times.

PART VI

How to Sell Your Plan: The Human "PERT Chart"

This part is truly the capstone to all that has gone before. Up to this point you have been shown why planning is important, how it can be used to enhance your position in the organization, and how to perform the three basic planning tasks that face business.

The last and final step will show you how to steer your plan through the organization labyrinth to obtain approval. It is assumed, of course, that you have violated none of the basic principles and that your plan is well thought out and documented.

Getting your plan over the successive organization hurdles is *the* most important point of this entire book. Even if all of the prerequisites were admirably achieved, failure to get approval to go ahead will reduce all of your prior effort to naught.

Realize right now, at the outset, that there are only two categories of people in your organization with whom you must deal. First there are those who can *help you,* in the sense that their approval is needed. Second, there is the group who can *hurt you.* These are the people whose approval is *not* necessary but who can, indirectly, influence people in the first group to withhold or even deny approval. To get your plan implemented you must deal differently with these two groups. It is necessary that you obtain the approval of your plan from the first group. But both your strategy and your tactics are different with regard to the second group. All you really need to do with the second group is to neutralize them—literally, make them neutral. You want them to forebear in the use of their power or influence to persuade a member of the first group to withhold or deny approval.

A

The "Approval Chain"

The first question to deal with is, "Who will be affected by the plan?" Carefully list all the individuals whose job will change, whose reporting relationship will change, whose empire will be enlarged or diminished, and so on. This analysis cannot be too detailed. Successful performance of this task is dependent upon the same quality required of a successful planner: anticipation!—the ability to foresee the effects of an action before that action is taken. The ability to detach yourself and place yourself as completely as possible in the other person's shoes is equally important. Try to see what he sees, feel what he feels, think what he thinks.

Poring over a list of potentially affected individuals is tiring, tedious work that requires sustained concentration. But again, these are the qualities required of a successful planner. Very few people have the stamina required to complete even this first step successfully. That's why there are so few very good planners, and so very few "movers and shakers."

The number of individuals analyzed should be proportional to the depth and breadth—the organizational scope—of the plan. Common sense? Yes, it certainly is. But this elementary rule is far too often ignored or given short shrift. If you are going to err in the definition of the perimeter of analysis, however, always err by including a few too many rather than a few too few.

The initial list must include all of the individuals designated in company policy or procedure manuals according to the type and importance of the plan. "Importance" here usually refers to the amount of dollars involved. The basic rule is always "relevance and significance." "Relevance" speaks to the natural or traditional oversight exercised. For example, only rarely does a controller have approval power over a research and development plan. He has input responsibility, but only in very unusual circumstances can he approve *or* disapprove.

"Significance" usually deals with the amounts of dollars involved. Again, except for rare cases, the general rule is that the larger the number of dollars involved, the higher in the organization must approval be obtained.

Searching out and identifying the individuals in the "approval chain" is only the first step. Next expand the ambit of your search to identify those outside of the "approval chain" who will also be affected and *rank them in order of their ability to exercise opposition,* ranging from comments at the water fountain, through memo-issuing, to being able (informally) to exercise veto power by ability to influence a key person in the "approval chain."

Inclusion of all of the affected individuals will test your knowledge not only of the business operation of your firm but also of the roles that individuals *really* play. Of course, start with the published Organization Chart. But go beyond it and try to draw up a "Power Chart." Ascertain as carefully as you can who really has and/or exercises the power. Pay special attention to the power centers affected by your plan.

After you have completed the lists of all involved or affected individuals, separate the individuals according to those whose approval is required and those whose approval is not required but whose opposition may lead to failure to obtain approval. Your task then becomes a matter of devising ways and means to obtain approval from those whose approval is required, and ways and means to ensure that those not formally in the "approval chain" who can adversely affect approval will refrain. The easier of the two, usually, is obtaining approval from those whose approval is required.

You will never submit a plan that adversely affects an individual in the formal "approval chain"—at least not overtly. To do so is tantamount to a palace revolt. Therefore, the key to analysis of the individuals in the formal approval chain is to examine each one by one to ascertain what characteristics, features, objectives, goals, or whatever will turn each one on, and then be sure to include them in your plan to the fullest applicable measure. The "hot buttons" can and do range all the way from good old reliable return on investment to "pizzazz" that can raise market price. They range from ego-building emotion to cold, hard-eyed financial results. While the "hot buttons" are not really difficult to determine, don't be lulled into doing an incomplete job because of the relative ease of the task.

B

The Approval/"Hot Button" Table

Formalize your analysis by completing an Approval/Hot Button Table. Call it a chart or matrix—it doesn't make any difference. The purpose of it *is* important. By relating the approval individual, in the lines, to the "hot buttons," in the columns, you can quickly gain an overview of the features, characteristics, and so forth that your plan will need to incorporate.

Not all "hot buttons" are equally "hot" to every individual. The degree of heat for any one "hot button" will vary from time to time as other conditions vary. Therefore, in the intersection of each Approval/Hot Button, assign your best guess number of the degree of heat existing at the time you pick for your plan submittal. Use a 0–10 rating scheme, where a 10 connotes the greatest heat. A 5 would mean that you estimate his interest to be only lukewarm. Refer often to your Hot Button Table.

Update it as you become aware of changes. This is *not* a one-time document!

You know, the odd thing about this whole subject is that people spend a lot of time on it. They talk about it, they speculate about it, and they gossip. Two observations should be made. First, for all the time they spend doing this type of analysis, they invariably do it *informally*. What a waste! They never keep a record of their data points. Consequently, they have great difficulty in trying to *use* the data to enrich their firm's future—and thereby their own!

The second observation is that almost everybody goes through this exercise *after the fact*. The conversation usually runs, "No wonder (this or that) happened and he reacted (this or that) way." The extensive prevalence of this "after the fact" analysis gives compelling credibility to the proposition that most of the people really don't have the vaguest idea about what *will happen* because of what a few rare, truly effective planners are up to!

Now comes the really tough part. What we have to do is deal with those individuals who are (1) *not* in the formal approval chain and (2) potentially capable of indirectly exercising veto power. Where does one begin? There are no company policy or procedure manuals that can tell you who these people are. There certainly is no published organization chart that can direct you to those individuals. You begin, simply, by yourself. This will be your most difficult, challenging task. It will measure your skill, talent and ability (1) to foresee and anticipate accurately, and (2) to project yourself into another's position.

The first step is somehow to identify who the individuals are who will be affected, whether favorably or otherwise, by this particular plan you seek to implement. There is only one sure way that this can be done. *Envision the plan already implemented.* Wave a mental magic wand and, lo and behold, the plan has been approved! What, then, are the consequences? What are the ripples? The side effects? Who has been touched?

As you make note of the answers to those questions, be mindful that what we're going to do is create a Veto Defense Table. It will resemble the Approval/Hot Button Table in that names of affected individuals will appear in the lines. The columns, however, will be headed by the various ways in which an individual *could* be affected—both favorably *and* unfavorably. Some examples: Empire will grow, empire will diminish; placed more in a superior role, more in a subordinate role; will be more visible/accountable, will be less visible/accountable; will have more/less responsibility; will/will not be likely to get a raise; and so on.

As you begin this analysis, don't forget for a moment that *you do not have to get the approval of these individuals! All you MUST do is get them to refrain from opposition. All they need to do, if you are to be successful, is to be INDIFFERENT!* This point is absolutely crucial. As you gain greater appreciation and understanding of this point, you will in turn gain greater appreciation and understanding of the concept of *"corridor of indifference."* The essence of this concept deals with your ability to steer a course for your plan that successfully avoids invocation of the veto.

What this step in the development of the Human PERT Chart is about is the definition of the corridor of indifference. Once you know the pitfalls along the route, it will be easier to avoid them. Your goal is to identify, *for each affected individual,* how he will view your plan in terms of likely outcomes for *him.* This step can never really be complete. A great deal depends upon the perception of the individual involved, in addition to your perception of his reaction.

C

The Veto Defense Index Table

Once the table is complete with respect to individuals and column headings (effects of your plan on that individual), the next step is to assign the Veto Defense Index. While a 0–10 value was useful in the Approval/Hot Button Table, such a value would be useless here. What we're looking for, remember, is to avoid "negatives" and somehow to get these individuals to at least a "zero" or neutral condition. So, the Veto Defense Index should be expressed in terms of −10 to +10. A −10 indicates that the effect of your plan on this individual would be devastating, and he would do all he could to thwart approval. At the other extreme, a +10 would signify your belief that this individual would positively support your plan because of its favorable effects on him.

Earlier I told you that the Approval/Hot Button Table should be drafted as soon as you join the organization and updated periodically. In the case of the Veto Defense

Index Table, however, this is an *ad hoc* exercise. Because it relates the effects of each specific plan on each individual affected, it must be prepared and evaluated *each time* a new plan is pondered.

Okay, now we've got both of our basic documents, the Approval/Hot Button Table and the Veto Defense Table. What do we do now? While it's disarmingly simple to state, it's exceedingly tough to do. First we devise an individualized, personalized plan of action to convert each Approval/Hot Button that we can from "zero" to as high a "plus" as we can. This may mean that we go "back to the drawing board" to see where and how we can include more or stronger Hot Button appeal in our plan. If the Hot Button is return on investment, maybe, upon closer inspection, it is possible to reduce research and development, to reduce working capital (inventories and accounts receivable) requirements, to accelerate sales, and so on. Maybe it is possible to lease on a short term rather than acquire fixed assets, thus lowering the investment. If the Hot Button is minimal exposure to downside risk, perhaps there are possibilities of increasing the number of abort decision steps at smaller increments of commitment. And so on. While it may superficially appear that all we're doing is catering to whims, prejudices, and convictions, the reality is that the plan itself is a stronger, more credible and viable plan! All that the Approval/Hot Button Table did for us was to force us to take into account those factors or criteria most important to those whose approval is necessary in the first place!

Now then, let us proceed to deal with the Veto Defense Index Table. Because this table can only be prepared anew as each new plan is formulated, additional analytical care is not only warranted, it is mandatory. The first step, of course, is to complete the table initially. After indexes have been entered in each of the intersections, the next step is to rank the entries in increasing absolute value. That is to say, all of the indexes should be ranked, irrespective of the ways an individual is affected and of the individual himself, in order of priority of correction or improvement. Thus, all those indexes whose value is −10 should top the list. Until you can find some way to reduce these −10s to zero or close to zero, there is no point in considering what to do about the −2s and −3s.

A cynical eye will view this exercise as a devising of palliatives, tossing a bone to the dogs. A professional eye, on the other hand, will see it as a bona fide, sure-fire way to unify the organization and to avoid morale problems. The net result, if this step is successfully performed, is that the likelihood of success of the entire plan has been dramatically enhanced. And the plan will have been implemented without the divisive and costly bickering and infighting too often seen when this exercise is ignored or slighted.

The time has now come to discuss how to deal with the individuals identified in your Approval/Hot Button and Veto Defense Index Tables. Before proceeding, it will be most helpful for you to review earlier portions of this book. In particular, review the principles in Part I and Part II, Section A, "The Nature of Organizational Power."

D

Negotiation (or Navigation)

Finished your review? The basics are fresh in your mind? Okay, let's talk for a bit about dealing one on one. What you're going to have to do with each identified individual, one by one, is *negotiate*. While a number of current books deal with this important subject, they are not really of much use to us for our purposes here. The critical difference is that in the "typical" negotiating situation, the parties on both sides are known to each other, *and* their adversarial relationship is mutually known when the negotiations begin.

In our context, however, the "other party" does *not* know that he's an adversary. Only *you* know what you're *planning* to do. What you must do is anticipate his concerns and reservations and mitigate them to acceptable or tolerable levels, so that interference with implementation of your plan is avoided. This initial situational relationship is particularly favorable. Successful dealing with the "other party" is enhanced, because he will not yet have taken a "position."

The traditional negotiating situation can be described as two parties, each with a definite "position" or set of objectives that is in conflict with the other. It is a "zero-sum" situation. That is, the benefit gained by achievement of one party's objectives represent a penalty or loss to the other party. Almost always, in the traditional negotiating situation, the respective positions taken at the outset only faultily mirror the *real* interests of the parties. In the traditional negotiating situation there are *two* levels of bargaining. First there are the openly stated issues or demands. Second there are the *"real"* interests of the parties, which are rarely, if ever, openly stated. In a buy-sell negotiation, for instance, neither party ever reveals his "real" number at the outset.

The greatest obstacle to reaching agreement is presented by the complications that arise from the openly stated issues, the announced objectives that each party seeks to achieve. The more that discussion centers on the objectives or ends that each seeks, the less chance there is for achieving effective resolution or agreement. Each tries to enhance or solidify his "position." The problem with this "positional bargaining" is that the discussion deteriorates to a contest of wills. The purpose of negotiating is *not* to win a "contest"! *The purpose of negotiating is to accommodate the parties' underlying real need to a changed set of circumstances.* Focus on "position"—that is, effort expended in the "clarification" of position, in defense of your position and attack on his—may lead to some kind of an "agreement." But that agreement will be short-lived. Only acceptance of the "letter" of the agreement will be grudgingly surrendered by the "loser." Noncompliance with the "spirit" of the agreement spells its early demise. You may have "won," but if you "won" at the cost of "loss of face" for your adversary, you will have won, in the final analysis, worse than nothing. You will not only have created an "enemy," you will also have chilled relationships with all others who will have learned of the manner in which you achieved "victory." They will forever thereafter view you with a wary eye.

All of these complications can be avoided when "negotiating" your plan through the Human PERT Chart! *You* know what your *real* interests are. To the extent that your analyses (Approval/Hot Button and Veto Defense Index tables) are thorough and insightful, you will have an understanding of *his real* interests if your plan is implemented. By careful analysis, you will have devised means to accommodate his *real* interest before he even feels that they may be jeopardy.

You can avoid entirely the artless ballet of position confrontation. You are in position to deal directly with the *real* interests of the parties *before* an adversarial relationship is established!

That is not to say that position issues will not emerge when your plan is unveiled. Of course they will. But they will fall like straw men and not leave relationship scars, insofar as you will have previously satisfied the *real* interests affected by the plan.

The most effective negotiations are, after all, one-party negotiations. By skillful use of No-Nonsense Planning, you can devise and *implement* plans—you can effect change, you can exercise organizational power—and all the while you can avoid two (or more) party negotiations! You can do it by anticipating the *real* interests of the affected individuals and avoiding damage to those interests before you take overt action, before you fully reveal or publish your plan.

Sure, it sounds easy. How in the world do you actually *do* it? Well, start out by remembering that the *real* interests of people listed in the Veto Defense Index Table need *not* be enhanced or enlarged. They need only be *not* damaged or diminished to the point where your target individual will be energized to oppose. The "negotiations" with these individuals may take considerable time and require numerous conversations. Generally speaking, the more minus the index the longer the duration of the negotiating process. Whatever his "real" interest, so long as it is a legitimate interest, there will always be offsetting factors that can be employed to avoid fatal damage. For example, if his *real* interest is job security, he must be persuaded that if the plan (or portion thereof) does in some way make him more "indispensable," his initial -8 may be reduced to a more acceptable -3 or -2.

Regardless, however, of the duration or the number of intermediary steps, the first step is always to establish a superior–subordinate relationship. The stronger the relationship the better, of course, but even a mild, temporary one will suffice. No one will ever be seriously susceptible to one-party negotiations unless they truly feel that you can or might help them, or can or might hurt them. So your first step is to condition that individual mentally to accept the likelihood that what you plan to do can or might affect one or more of his *real* interests. You must speak to that individual's needs, hopes, aspirations, and dreams. It is in those areas that *real* interests *really* lie. He must be made to feel that the likelihood is real to advance his *real* interests, or at least that they are not endangered.

All the succeeding steps are aimed at conditioning his organizational behavior. That's another way of saying that you exercise power over him. The extent to which you can accurately become aware of his perceptions and *real* interests, and the extent to which he feels that you can or might help or hurt those *real* interests, is the precise extent to which his organizational behavior can be controlled and predicted.

All well and good, you say, but suppose I run into an individual who simply cannot, for any number of reasons—lack of accessibility is the most frequently named—be conditioned into a superior–subordinate relationship? What, then, do I do? How do I proceed?

Panic not! There *is* another time-tested, proven way. Let's explain it in a C-B-A No-Nonsense Planning sequence. Ability to control and predict organizational behavior is a manifestation of organizational power. The measure of the power you exercise is the extent to which he feels a commitment to the plan. In turn, the measure of his commitment is the extent to which he feels he has a "stake" in the plan. Continuing, the measure of his "stake" in the plan is the extent to which he feels (or is) involved in the undertaking. In an A-B-C sequence, merely let him "participate" in the plan. In other words, let him have a "piece of the action." The approach is first to convince (*not* persuade) him of the importance, immediacy, and likelihood of success of the plan. Predetermine the role you want him to play, the extent to which you want him to participate. Then lead him to that role, to that extent of participation.

You want to get him to "invest" his time and talent in the plan. Once you get him to make the investment, he will be amenable to compromise. In fact, the degree of willingness to compromise in a negotiation is always in direct proportion to the extent of the investment that has been made.

While this form of "participatory management" is always available as a Veto Defense technique, it is also always less preferable than the one-party negotiation technique. The goal of a one-party negotiation is to mollify concern over jeopardy to "real" interests while keeping intact the elements and provisions of the plan. Whenever participation in the preparation of the plan occurs, the plan elements and provisions are thereby affected. Thus great care must be exercised to ensure that the substance and essentials of your plan are not fragmented and obliterated by negotiation compromise with too many plan definition participants.

As a safeguard, if your analysis convinces you that participation (that is, plan modification) will be required, include in your original formulation plan provisions and elements that you will be willing to modify or even remove later during participatory negotiations. Just as a seller always starts with a price somewhat higher than the price he is really willing to accept, try to include provisions, initially, that represent greater adverse impact on your negotiating partner. Thus, as discussions proceed you can relinquish some ground without damaging the plan you really seek to implement.

Index